The Bc

Risk Management In Payments

Navigating Threats, Trust, and Transformation in the Digital Payments Ecosystem

The Book On Series

By David Webb

Published by The Book On Publishing, 2025.
First Edition. May 6, 2025.
Website: https://thebookon.ca
Substack: https://thebookonpublishing.substack.com/

While every precaution has been taken in the preparation of this book, the publisher assumes no responsibility for errors or omissions, or damages resulting from the use of the information contained herein.

RISK MANAGEMENT IN PAYMENTS: Navigating Threats, Trust, and Transformation in the Digital Payments Ecosystem

First Edition. May 6, 2025.

Copyright © 2025 The Book On Publishing

ISBN: 978-1-997795-70-4

Written by David Webb.

The Book On Series

The Book On Life Unscripted
The Book On Risk Management in Payments
The Book On AI for Everyday People
The Book On Relationships
The Book On Mastering The Algorithm
The Book On Saying No
The Book On Community-Led Strategy
The Book On The Myth of Multitasking
The Book On The Burnout Blueprint
The Book On The Digital Reboot
The Book On The Shape of What's Coming
The Book On Strategic Obsession
The Book On High-Stakes Thinking
The Book On Artificial Leverage
The Book On Clarity
The Book On Uncertainty
The Book On Operational Excellence
The Book On Escape
The Book On Reinvention After Consequences
The Book On Re-Unifying Society
The Book On Taking Flight
The Book On Persuasion
The Book On Enough
The Book On Attention
The Book On Men (for Women)
The Book On Women (for Men)
The Book On The Cookbook for Cannibals
The Book On Woke
The Book On BS
The Book On GenZ Survival Mode

Table of Contents

Dedication

To my wife, Robbin
Your unwavering love, strength, and patience
They were with me through every trial and triumph.
You stood by my side as I navigated the uncharted waters.
of being a first mover in the payments industry.
This book, like so many milestones in my life,
wouldn't exist without you.

David

Read This First

This is not a book designed to entertain you. It's not here to charm, to soothe, or to hold your hand. It won't dazzle you with stories, metaphors, or motivational fluff. What you're having is a tool, an instruction manual written for people who are serious about learning, executing, and thinking at a higher level.

Every book in The Book On Series is built on a single premise: clarity beats complexity. We believe that when you strip away the noise, the emotions, the marketing spin, and the cultural rituals of "self-help," what's left is raw, unembellished instruction. That's what these books offer.

They are dry by design. Not because we don't care about language or narrative, but because when you're building something that matters, you don't need more distractions. You need a clear architecture. Mental scaffolding. Direction that respects your intelligence.

Each title in this series takes on a specific domain: decision-making, clarity, strategy, leverage, and uncertainty, and drills deep, not in over-generalizations, but in applied frameworks. These are books for builders, operators, founders, tacticians, and thinkers—people who don't just consume knowledge but operationalize it.

You'll find no chapter-long anecdotes here. No self-congratulatory memoirs. No bullet-point platitudes. Instead, what you'll get is structured insight: argument, example, application. The tone is direct. The prose is sober. The ideas are designed to be lifted out and used.

You won't be coddled, but you won't be misled either.

There's a place in the world for lyrical, emotional, story-driven books, and this isn't that place. This is a workspace. A blueprint. A conversation for people who are ready to act, not just absorb.

We respect your time and your intellect.

Welcome to The Book On Series.

Introduction

Why Risk Management is the Backbone of Modern Payment

Whether it's a tap at the checkout counter, an online subscription renewal, or a cross-border wire transfer, every transaction triggers a complex sequence of behind-the-scenes processes. In today's digital economy, speed and security are no longer optional. At the heart of this financial choreography lies one essential discipline: risk management.

Payments are the lifeblood of global commerce. As technology accelerates the speed and scale of financial transactions, the opportunities for innovation have never been greater, but so too are the threats. From fraud and cyberattacks to regulatory scrutiny and operational failures, the risks surrounding payments are more diverse and sophisticated than ever before. In this environment, a reactive stance is no longer sufficient. Companies must anticipate, assess, and proactively mitigate risks in real time, or risk being left behind.

Risk management is not just a function reserved for compliance teams or auditors. It is the strategic foundation upon which resilient, scalable, and trusted payment systems are built. It guides product development, informs customers onboarding, shapes security protocols, and ensures alignment with global regulatory frameworks. In a space where trust is currency, effective risk management becomes a competitive advantage.

This book explores how modern payment companies, from traditional banks to agile fintechs, are rethinking risk in an era defined by innovation and volatility. It provides a roadmap for navigating uncertainty, building robust frameworks, and embedding risk awareness into the DNA of any organization operating in the payments space.

Whether you're an executive looking to strengthen your company's defenses, a compliance officer refining your risk program, or a startup founder trying to scale safely, this book will equip you with the insights and tools needed to thrive in a high-stakes, high-speed ecosystem.

Because in the world of payments, you're not just moving money, you're managing trust. And trust, above all, must be protected.

The Evolution of the Payments Industry

Over the past two decades, the payments industry has undergone a dramatic transformation, evolving from slow, paper-based processes to an ecosystem of instant, invisible, and borderless digital transactions. What was once dominated by cash, checks, and manual bank transfers is now an intricate web of APIs, real-time payment rails, mobile wallets, and blockchain-based systems.

This revolution has been driven by three converging forces: technology, consumer demand, and regulatory pressure. Technology has become more innovative every day. Consumers have demanded convenience, speed, and seamless experiences. Regulators, in turn, have pushed for tighter controls, transparency, and anti-fraud measures to keep pace with the changing landscape.

As a result, the payments industry no longer operates in silos. Traditional banks now coexist with fintech startups, neobanks, Big Tech, and decentralized platforms. Payment service providers (PSPs), acquirers, and gateways must navigate a fragmented and hyper-competitive marketplace, where partnerships and platform integrations are essential for survival. But with this opportunity comes complexity, and with complexity, risk.

Each innovation introduces new vulnerabilities. The shift to contactless payments, embedded finance, and Buy Now, Pay Later (BNPL) models bring heightened exposure to identity fraud, credit risk, and transaction laundering. The rise of cryptocurrencies and decentralized finance (DeFi) challenges traditional risk models and regulatory frameworks. Meanwhile, the globalization of commerce introduces compliance challenges across jurisdictions with conflicting rules and enforcement standards.

Moreover, fraudsters have evolved just as quickly. Armed with AI, stolen credentials, and dark web marketplaces, they exploit weak points in the payment chain, whether it's a phishing attack on a customer or an API vulnerability in a fintech stack. The line between cyber risk and payment risk has blurred, forcing organizations to adopt a more integrated, real-time approach to threat detection and response.

This chapter will explore the historical milestones that brought us here, the key inflection points that accelerated change, and the emerging risk trends that every player in the ecosystem must prepare for. Understanding this evolution is not just a matter of perspective; it's a prerequisite for building resilient, forward-looking risk strategies in an industry where change is the only constant.

Who This Book Is For

The payments industry is no longer a niche function tucked behind banking systems; it has become one of the most visible and consequential engines of the global economy. This book is written for those navigating that reality from every corner of the ecosystem.

If you're a compliance officer or risk manager, you're already at the forefront of regulatory enforcement and fraud defense. But today's threat landscape demands more than checklists. It demands adaptable frameworks, real-time decision-making, and a culture that sees risk not as a bottleneck, but as a form of protection and strategy.

If you're building the next great fintech startup, this book will help you scale responsibly. It's not about slowing down innovation; it's about ensuring that speed doesn't outrun security. From onboarding flows to transaction monitoring, you'll gain tools to embed trust into your product from day one.

If you operate within a payment service provider, acquirer, or ISO, your position in the value chain brings a unique challenge: inheriting risk from both upstream and downstream. Here, you'll learn how to evaluate merchant behavior, manage partner exposure, and stay resilient in a competitive, fragmented market.

Regulators and policymakers will also find value here. This book offers a practical lens into how modern platforms operate, where real-world gaps exist, and how regulation must evolve alongside innovation, not lag it.

And if you're a cybersecurity or fraud analyst, this book connects your work to the broader architecture of payments. It helps you understand how data, behavior, infrastructure, and intent intersect, and how to stay a step ahead of those exploiting that intersection.

Ultimately, this book is for anyone whose work touches how money moves: technologists, strategists, product leads, banking professionals, and anyone responsible for trust in a digital-first economy. Because today, risk isn't just a support function, it's part of your competitive edge.

Section 1: Understanding the Landscape

Chapter 1: The Modern Payments Ecosystem

The modern payments ecosystem is one of the most complex, dynamic, and critical infrastructures in our global economy. What once existed as a tightly controlled network dominated by a few banks and card associations has evolved into a sprawling, interconnected system, one that supports trillions of dollars in digital commerce, spans countless intermediaries, and now moves at the speed of real time.

Briefly, a payment may be simply a transfer of money from one account to another, fast, invisible, and frictionless. But behind every tap, click, or swipe lies a dense chain of infrastructure, legal agreements, regulatory oversight, risk controls, and commercial logic. Each player in the process, from the merchant to the card network, the processor to the issuing bank, plays a distinct and indispensable role in ensuring that value moves not just efficiently, but safely and compliantly.

Powerful trends have shaped this ecosystem. Technological innovation has driven down barriers to entry. Regulatory modernization has allowed new business models to flourish. And consumer demand for convenience, speed, and trust has forced even the most traditional institutions to adapt or be left behind.

As the ecosystem has expanded, so has its surface area for risk. More players mean more potential points of failure. Faster transactions mean less time to detect fraud. New technologies introduce new vulnerabilities. And as the ecosystem decentralizes, accountability becomes harder to define, and even harder to enforce.

Understanding the anatomy of this system is a prerequisite for managing its risks. This chapter provides a structural map of the modern payments landscape, not just who the players are, but how they interconnect, where responsibility sits, and how money moves from payer to payee. By demystifying the system, we lay the foundation for deeper discussions on risk exposure, regulatory pressure, and strategic resilience that follow in the rest of this book.

Key Players in the Modern Payments Ecosystem

To effectively manage risk in payments, you need to understand who the stakeholders are and what roles they play. Each participant introduces its vulnerabilities and controls, and no transaction is truly isolated. The following outlines the most critical actors:

Card Networks

Card networks, such as Visa, Mastercard, American Express, and Discover, are often the most recognizable brands in the payments industry, yet their role is frequently misunderstood. Contrary to popular belief, these networks do not issue credit cards or provide lending services directly to consumers. Instead, they operate as orchestrators of a global payment system, managing the infrastructure, rules, and settlement processes that allow billions of transactions to occur between consumers, merchants, and financial institutions.

At their core, card networks serve as neutral intermediaries. They connect issuing banks (those that provide cards to consumers) with acquiring banks (those that enable merchants to accept cards). Every time a consumer makes a card payment, whether online, in-store, or through a mobile wallet, the card network facilitates the communication and processing required to authorize and settle that transaction.

Their responsibilities are multifaceted. They define the technical specifications for transaction messaging, implement security standards such as EMV (chip cards) and tokenization protocols, and enforce operational rules around chargebacks, refunds, and dispute resolution. They also play a pivotal role in network-level risk management, monitoring patterns across all transactions flowing through their systems to detect anomalies, prevent fraud, and protect the integrity of the ecosystem.

Importantly, the networks do not carry financial risk associated with transactions. That burden rests with the issuing and acquiring banks, but the network ensures that risk is measured and managed consistently across all participants. This makes the network a kind of "rule maker and referee," responsible for balancing fairness, speed, and security among stakeholders with sometimes conflicting interests.

In addition to their traditional roles, card networks have become platform innovators. Visa and Mastercard, for example, have made strategic acquisitions and launched APIs to support real-time payments, token services, open banking, and digital identity. Their ambition is no longer to facilitate card transactions; it's to become the backbone of global digital commerce, beyond cards.

For risk professionals, understanding card networks is critical because many downstream controls, such as dispute processes, merchant monitoring, and even fraud scoring, are shaped by rules the networks enforce globally. Non-compliance with these rules can result in fines, revocation of processing privileges, or reputational damage. Meanwhile, innovations at the network level, such as changes to authorization logic or updates to fraud frameworks, ripple out across the industry, often requiring rapid adaptation by PSPs, banks, and fintechs alike.

In short, card networks are the invisible rails behind most consumer payments, powerful, pervasive, and constantly evolving. Their influence on both the mechanics and governance of payments cannot be overstated.

Issuing and Acquiring Banks

While card networks provide the connective infrastructure for global payments, it is the issuing and acquiring banks that shoulder most of the operational, financial, and compliance responsibilities behind each transaction. These banks don't just move money; they underwrite, authorize, and ultimately own the financial risk that comes with it.

Let's start with issuing banks. These are the institutions that provide payment cards to consumers or businesses. When you receive a credit or debit card with a Visa or Mastercard logo, it is the issuer, not the network, that extends the line of credit, manages your billing cycle, and oversees collections or customer disputes. Issuers approve or decline transactions in real time based on available funds, risk models, and customer behavior. They are the first line of defense against fraudulent activity, leveraging both network data and proprietary analytics to make authorization decisions.

Issuers also play a key role in regulatory compliance, ensuring that their onboarding and transaction monitoring systems meet requirements for KYC (Know Your Customer), AML (Anti-Money Laundering), and consumer protection standards. In many regions, they are supervised by both banking regulators and payments oversight bodies, requiring them to balance innovation with robust controls.

On the other side of the transaction is the acquiring bank, also known as the "merchant acquirer." These banks enable businesses to accept card payments by providing them with merchant accounts. An acquirer settles payments with the merchant, manages chargebacks and reversals, and facilitates communication with the card network and issuing bank. They are also responsible for underwriting the merchant relationship, assessing the merchant's risk level based on industry, sales volume, refund rates, and compliance with network rules.

Acquirers must monitor for signs of merchant fraud, money laundering, or misuse of the payment system. High-risk verticals, such as adult content, supplements, or travel, often require enhanced scrutiny. Failure to detect and address violations can result in fines from card networks, as well as increased reserve requirements or even termination from the ecosystem.

It's worth noting that many banks function as both issuers and acquirers. Some of the largest financial institutions in the world, including JPMorgan Chase, Citi, and Bank of America, operate at both ends of the transaction flow. This gives them visibility across the entire lifecycle of a payment and allows for more integrated risk controls.

For newer entrants, such as fintechs and payment facilitators, access to these bank functions typically happens through sponsorships or partnerships. A startup may offer a digital wallet or branded debit card, but behind the scenes, a licensed bank issues the card and holds the regulatory responsibility.

Ultimately, issuing and acquiring banks are the financial lungs of the payments system. They extend credit, absorb chargeback risk, fund settlements, and ensure compliance across diverse markets and use cases. For any payment platform operating at scale, maintaining strong relationships with these banks and understanding their risk frameworks is essential to long-term viability.

Payment Service Providers (PSPs)

In the era of digital commerce, Payment Service Providers (PSPs) have become essential infrastructure, not just for merchants, but for the entire payment ecosystem. Platforms like Stripe, Adyen, Checkout.com, and Square have redefined how businesses accept payments by offering a fully integrated solution that bundles everything from onboarding and authorization to fraud screening, settlement, and reporting.

Where traditional acquirers focused on large merchants and complex integrations, PSPs emerged to serve a broader market, particularly startups, platforms, and small to mid-sized businesses. Their appeal lies in abstraction: merchants no longer need to manage separate relationships with banks, gateways, and fraud vendors. Instead, they access a streamlined, developer-friendly interface that oversees everything in one place.

But with simplification comes complexity, especially in risk management.

PSPs often function as aggregators, pooling multiple sub-merchants under a single master account. While this model speeds onboarding and supports rapid scaling, it also introduces portfolio-level risk. A single bad merchant can jeopardize the PSP's standing with card networks or sponsor banks, especially if fraud or chargeback thresholds are breached.

To mitigate this, leading PSPs invest heavily in automated risk engines that assess merchant risk at onboarding and continuously monitor behavior post-activation. Sophisticated PSPs employ layered controls: velocity checks, device fingerprinting, behavioral analytics, and adaptive transaction scoring. Some use tiered risk models that dynamically adjust funding timelines, reserve requirements, or approval thresholds based on evolving risk signals.

PSPs also face pressure from both directions in the ecosystem. On one side, card networks and acquiring banks hold them accountable for sub-merchant behavior, requiring transparency, registration, and compliance with operating rules. On the other hand, merchants demand instant onboarding and frictionless payments, creating tension between risk controls and user experience.

Beyond processing, many PSPs now offer value-added services: working capital advances, embedded wallets, currency conversion, fraud APIs, and reconciliation tools. Each of these brings new regulatory exposure, from lending compliance to cross-border transaction monitoring, expanding the PSP's risk surface.

For risk professionals, PSPs represent both a powerful enabler and a potential bottleneck. Their role at the center of the modern payments stack means that breakdowns, whether technical, operational, or compliance-related, can have ripple effects across thousands of merchants and millions of transactions.

Ultimately, PSPs have redefined what it means to be a payments provider. They offer speed, flexibility, and scale, but maintaining trust and compliance at that speed requires deep integration of risk management into every layer of their platforms.

Independent Sales Organizations (ISOs)

Before the rise of digital-native PSPs and automated onboarding, many merchants entered the payments ecosystem through Independent Sales Organizations (ISOs). These third-party entities resell merchant services on behalf of acquiring banks or processors. While often operating under the branding of their sponsor acquirers, ISOs function with significant autonomy, managing their own sales pipelines, agent networks, and merchant portfolios.

ISOs primarily serve as distribution engines. They find and sign merchants, assist with onboarding, and often provide first-line customer support. In many markets, particularly among small businesses, restaurants, and service providers, ISOs still maintain strong relationships and local market insight that larger PSPs may lack.

But this decentralized model also introduces inherent risk. ISOs are typically removed from the core compliance and underwriting functions of the acquirer or PSP they represent. This creates a layer of separation, one where risk oversight is less direct, and incentives may be misaligned. A sales agent, for example, might be motivated to onboard a merchant quickly to earn commission, even if that merchant raises red flags in a standard risk review.

Historically, ISOs have been a common entry point for high-risk or misclassified merchants. In some cases, this has included deliberate violations like merchant laundering, where a seemingly legitimate business processes transactions on behalf of a prohibited or hidden entity. Even when misconduct is unintentional, inadequate due diligence can lead to elevated chargebacks, regulatory scrutiny, and fines from card networks.

To address this, card brands like Visa and Mastercard require formal ISO registration, and acquiring banks are expected to monitor ISO performance. This includes periodic audits, residual analysis, and portfolio-level risk reviews. Acquirers are ultimately liable for the merchants ISOs bring into the ecosystem, even if those merchants were never directly underwritten by the bank itself.

Some ISOs have evolved beyond simple sales roles. Larger, more sophisticated ISOs may now offer hardware provisioning, value-added services, or integrated POS systems, blurring the line between ISO and full-service payment provider. While this evolution increases their relevance, it also broadens their risk profile, requiring enhanced operational controls, customer verification, and technology governance.

For modern payment platforms, ISOs present a strategic trade-off. They offer reach, agility, and local expertise, but they also introduce fragmentation and potential blind spots. Any organization that relies on ISO partnerships must treat them as critical extensions of their risk perimeter, not just sales channels, but operational entities that need oversight, training, and ongoing risk alignment.

Fintechs and Embedded Payments

Over the past decade, fintechs have rapidly reshaped the financial landscape by integrating payments into products, platforms, and services where consumers already engage. Rather than building standalone financial institutions, many of these companies have adopted an embedded payments model, integrating financial functionality into digital experiences such as ride-sharing apps, e-commerce platforms, subscription services, and payroll tools.

What makes embedded payments so powerful is their invisibility. Users don't think about moving money; they tap, click, or receive. The payment becomes part of the flow, seamless, contextual, and frictionless. This shift in behavior creates immense user value but also introduces new forms of risk that are less visible and harder to control.

Most fintechs are not licensed financial institutions. Instead, they operate through sponsorships and infrastructure partnerships, connecting with banks, processors, and compliance vendors to deliver regulated services behind the scenes. For example, a neobank may use a Banking-as-a-Service (BaaS) provider to issue cards and store funds, while relying on an external PSP for transaction processing and a third-party vendor for KYC verification.

This layered model accelerates time to market but also diffuses accountability. When something goes wrong, a fraud event, compliance violation, or system outage, determining where responsibility lies can be challenging. A missed alert in a KYC vendor's pipeline might result in onboarding a fraudulent user, yet the fintech, not the vendor, may bear the regulatory consequences.

The pace of growth often exacerbates this risk. Many fintechs scale faster than their compliance or risk functions can mature. A successful product launch might drive thousands of new users overnight, straining identity verification systems, transaction monitoring capacity, and customer support. In such scenarios, controls can lag demand, opening the door to systemic vulnerabilities.

Fintechs also tend to serve underserved or edge-case markets, gig workers, underbanked users, or microbusinesses, where traditional credit and identity data are limited. This makes fraud detection more difficult and often necessitates alternative risk modeling, behavioral analytics, or manual review layers.

Regulators have taken notice. In many regions, fintechs are now required to register as financial entities, even if their core services are outsourced. Open banking initiatives, digital identity laws, and real-time payments mandates are pulling fintechs into the regulatory spotlight, whether they anticipated it or not.

From a risk perspective, embedded payments are highly efficient but structurally exposed. The abstraction that delights users also masks where vulnerabilities reside. Fintechs that succeed over the long term are those that embed compliance and risk management as profoundly as they embed their APIs, not as an afterthought, but as part of the product itself.

As the financial stack becomes more composable, embedded, and decentralized, the companies at the forefront of innovation must ensure that trust and oversight scale just as fast as user adoption. Because in a world where every app can become a bank, every product becomes a payments platform, and every team becomes a risk team.

Transaction Lifecycle Overview

Every digital payment, whether it's a tap of a card, a mobile checkout, or a recurring subscription, follows a precise, multi-step journey behind the scenes. What feels instant to the end user is a coordinated series of actions involving multiple players across the payments ecosystem. Understanding this transaction lifecycle is fundamental to understanding where risks live and who owns them.

It begins with the cardholder, the consumer, initiating the transaction. They may swipe a card, enter their details into a checkout form, or authenticate via a mobile wallet. That payment information is first captured and securely encrypted by a payment gateway or terminal provider, then routed through a Payment Service Provider (PSP) or directly to an acquiring bank, depending on the setup.

The acquirer then forwards the transaction request to the appropriate card network, Visa, Mastercard, American Express, or others. The card network acts as a switchboard, routing the request to the issuing bank that issued the card. The issuer evaluates the transaction in real time: verifying the cardholder's identity, checking for available funds or credit, and running fraud and behavioral checks. If all criteria are met, the transaction is approved. If something looks suspicious, such as mismatched device data, location anomalies, or spending irregularities, the issuer may flag or decline it.

That decision, approve or decline, travels back along the same path: issuer to network, network to acquirer, acquirer to merchant. All of this typically happens in less than two seconds.

But that's only authorization.

After authorization, the transaction enters the clearing and settlement phase. This is where funds are moved. Over the next 24 to 72 hours (sometimes faster), the issuing bank releases funds to the card network, which transfers them to the acquiring bank. The acquirer then deposits the funds into the merchant's account, typically minus processing fees, reserve requirements, and any other applicable deductions.

Throughout this lifecycle, different players assume different types of risk. If fraud occurs, the financial loss may fall on the issuer, acquirer, merchant, or even the consumer, depending on where and how the fraud occurred. In card-present transactions, issuers generally assume liability. But in card-not-present environments (like e-commerce), the burden often shifts to the merchant unless they've implemented fraud prevention tools like 3D Secure.

Other risks emerge from the infrastructure itself. A gateway outage may prevent transaction authorization. A lag in fraud detection could allow repeat attacks. A mismatch in merchant classification might cause chargeback disputes to fall through the cracks. If the clearing process fails, the merchant may not receive funds on time, disrupting cash flow and eroding trust.

Understanding this lifecycle is more than technical fluency; it's a risk mapping exercise. Each step in the flow represents a potential point of failure, a surface for fraud, or an opportunity to enhance control. For risk professionals, mapping this journey is the first step in building systems that are both resilient and scalable.

Because in payments, it's not just about whether money moves, it's about how it moves, who moves it, and what happens when something goes wrong.

Most Widely Used Rails

ACH (Automated Clearing House) – United States

ACH is the backbone of non-urgent, account-to-account payments in the United States. Introduced in the 1970s as a more efficient, cost-effective alternative to paper checks, it remains a foundational payment rail in the U.S. financial system. The network is overseen by NACHA, in partnership with the Federal Reserve, and is responsible for moving trillions of dollars annually.

Its most common uses include payroll deposits, mortgage payments, utility bills, business-to-business invoicing, and tax refunds. These transactions are processed in batches, rather than in real time, with most clearing once or twice per business day. While standard ACH transfers typically settle within one to two business days, the system has evolved to support same-day ACH for certain transactions, albeit with dollar limits and cutoff windows.

Despite these improvements, ACH is not designed for time-sensitive payments or situations where immediate confirmation is required. The availability of funds can vary depending on the receiving bank, and the batch-based structure makes it less responsive than modern real-time systems.

Even so, ACH remains deeply entrenched in the U.S. economy. Its low cost, broad adoption, and reliability have made it indispensable, though its architecture still reflects a slower, pre-digital financial era.

FedNow – United States

FedNow is the U.S. Federal Reserve's long-anticipated leap into real-time payments. Launched in 2023, it provides instant clearing and settlement of payments between participating banks, 24 hours a day, 365 days a year. Unlike ACH, which relies on batch processing and delayed settlement, FedNow is designed for speed, certainty, and modern use cases.

Its core purpose is to serve as public infrastructure for time-sensitive transactions. Individuals can use it to send money instantly between bank accounts, while businesses can leverage it for just-in-time payments, emergency disbursements, or real-time invoicing. For financial institutions, it offers a way to meet rising consumer expectations without relying solely on private networks.

Each FedNow transaction settles in real time; funds are debited from the sender and credited to the recipient immediately, with finality. There are no overnight delays, no business-hour restrictions, and no uncertainty about when money will arrive.

However, FedNow's adoption is still in its early stages. Participation is voluntary, and while many banks are beginning to integrate it, broad consumer access will depend on how quickly financial institutions build the necessary front-end experiences.

FedNow positions itself as a digital-era alternative to ACH, one built for speed, transparency, and inclusivity. Its potential lies not only in the technology itself, but in how banks, platforms, and fintechs use it to reimagine money movement in real time.

RTP (Real-Time Payments) – United States

RTP, developed and operated by The Clearing House (TCH), was the United States' first real-time payments infrastructure explicitly built for the digital age. Launched in 2017, RTP enables 24/7/365 clearing and settlement of payments between participating financial institutions, with funds transferred and confirmed in seconds.

Unlike ACH or wire transfers, RTP was designed from the ground up for immediacy and transparency. When a payment is sent via RTP, both the sender and recipient receive instant confirmation. There are no settlement delays; the transaction is final the moment it's approved.

RTP is used across a growing range of scenarios, including instant payroll, insurance disbursements, B2B payments, and consumer-to-business transactions. The system also supports additional functionality, such as request-for-payment messages and rich data exchange, allowing financial institutions and platforms to build more dynamic user experiences on top of the rail.

One key distinction is that RTP is a private network, owned and operated by The Clearing House, a consortium of large U.S. banks. Participation has grown steadily, but unlike FedNow, which is publicly operated, RTP adoption has been somewhat shaped by commercial priorities and bank readiness.

Still, RTP has carved out a strong foothold in the U.S. payments landscape. It offers speed, certainty, and real-time communication between counterparties, all essential features in an economy that increasingly expects money to move as fast as data.

CHIPS (Clearing House Interbank Payments System) – United States

CHIPS is the backbone of high-value wire payments in the United States. Operated by The Clearing House, it processes large-dollar, time-critical transactions between financial institutions, particularly for corporate, interbank, and international payments.

Unlike ACH or consumer-focused rails, CHIPS is optimized for scale and liquidity efficiency. It settles fewer transactions than ACH but manages far more value, typically in the trillions of dollars per day. Payments processed through CHIPS are often used for things like securities settlements, commercial lending, syndicated loans, and FX transactions.

CHIPS operates as a net settlement system, meaning payments are queued and offset against each other throughout the day to minimize the amount of liquidity each bank must contribute. This design allows for efficient use of funds and faster throughput, while still ensuring that payments are final and irrevocable once processed.

Although it's not real-time in the retail sense, CHIPS is extremely fast and reliable. Transactions are generally settled within minutes and supported by strong controls for risk mitigation and message integrity.

Large, globally active banks primarily use CHIPS; it's not a consumer-facing network, but its role is essential. It provides the infrastructure that underpins many of the world's most critical financial flows, connecting the U.S. to the broader global payment ecosystem.

Fedwire – United States

Fedwire is the Federal Reserve's real-time gross settlement (RTGS) system for large-value payments. It is one of the most critical components of the U.S. financial system, used by banks, businesses, and government agencies to move funds securely and with finality.

Unlike batch-based systems like ACH or liquidity-optimized systems like CHIPS, Fedwire processes each payment individually and in real time. The moment a payment is sent through Fedwire, it is settled directly between participating institutions using central bank money, with no delay, no netting, and no reversal.

Fedwire is typically used for high-priority transactions were timing and certainty matter most. These include interbank transfers, settlement of Treasury securities, corporate disbursements, tax payments, and large commercial transactions. Because payments are irrevocable once processed, Fedwire offers the highest level of finality available in the U.S. system.

Operational hours are extensive, typically from early morning until the evening on business days, though not 24/7. Still, within those hours, payments move instantly. Each message includes structured fields for routing, reference data, and settlement instructions, making the system precise but also somewhat complex to integrate with.

While not built for everyday consumer use, Fedwire plays a foundational role in supporting both the domestic and cross-border flows that underpin the U.S. economy. Its combination of speed, finality, and central bank backing makes it the payment rail of choice for institutions that cannot afford uncertainty.

Faster Payments – United Kingdom

Faster Payments is the United Kingdom's real-time payment rail for low- and mid-value transactions. Introduced in 2008, it was one of the earliest nationwide systems to offer near-instant transfers between banks, and it remains a critical part of the UK's financial infrastructure today.

Faster Payments is designed for speed and flexibility. Most payments clear and settle within seconds, 24 hours a day, 7 days a week. The system supports a wide range of use cases, from person-to-person transfers and bill payments to business disbursements and supplier invoices.

The rail is open to a broad set of participants, including banks, building societies, and approved non-bank providers. This openness has made it a popular choice for fintechs offering instant bank-to-bank transfers and embedded payment flows. It has also helped standardize the user experience across banks, with consistent expectations around speed and confirmation.

While the service was initially limited to smaller payments, the cap has steadily increased over time. Today, most UK banks allow individual payments of up to £1 million via Faster Payments, enough to cover everything from payroll to property transactions.

That said, Faster Payments wasn't designed for complex transactions like FX settlement, securities clearing, or very high-value transfers. For those, CHAPS, the UK's high-value system, still plays a key role. And while Faster Payments is fast, it doesn't yet support the kind of enriched messaging or request-for-payment capabilities found in newer systems like RTP or FedNow.

Still, for most domestic UK payments, Faster Payments is the default. It delivers speed, certainty, and scale, with a proven track record of reliability, and serves as a strong model for other markets moving toward real-time rails.

PIX – Brazil

PIX is Brazil's instant payment system, launched by the Central Bank of Brazil in 2020, and it has quickly redefined how money moves in one of Latin America's largest economies. Unlike many payment systems driven by banks or private networks, PIX was developed and is actively managed by the country's central bank, a bold move aimed at democratizing financial access and reducing reliance on cash.

What sets PIX apart is its ubiquity and simplicity. Anyone with a bank account, from individuals to businesses, can send or receive funds instantly using just a phone number, email, tax ID, or a scannable QR code. Payments are processed 24/7, with immediate settlement and confirmation, even on weekends or holidays.

Adoption has been explosive. Within its first year, PIX became the dominant method for peer-to-peer transfers and gained traction in e-commerce, gig economy payouts, utility payments, and even government disbursements. Part of its appeal lies in the cost: most PIX transactions are free for individuals and priced competitively for businesses, making it especially attractive for micro-merchants and underserved populations.

PIX has also catalyzed financial inclusion. Many Brazilians who were previously unbanked now have access to real-time payments through digital wallets and simplified onboarding flows. The Central Bank has actively promoted interoperability and competition, allowing banks, fintechs, and neobanks to participate on equal terms.

While PIX is still evolving, its impact has already been profound. It's not just a payment rail, it's a national infrastructure play, combining central bank oversight with real-time technology to unlock faster, cheaper, and more inclusive financial services across the economy.

UPI (Unified Payments Interface) – India

UPI, or Unified Payments Interface, is India's flagship real-time payment system, and one of the most ambitious digital financial infrastructures in the world. Launched in 2016 by the National Payments Corporation of India (NPCI), UPI has transformed how Indians send, receive, and manage money, both online and offline.

UPI is designed for interoperability. It links bank accounts, digital wallets, and mobile apps through a single, unified platform that allows users to move money instantly using phone numbers, virtual payment addresses (like email-style aliases), QR codes, or biometric authentication. Whether you're paying a shopkeeper, splitting a restaurant bill, or transferring funds to family, UPI offers one of the fastest and simplest experiences anywhere.

What makes UPI incredibly powerful is its open architecture. Banks, fintechs, and third-party apps like Google Pay, PhonePe, and Paytm all operate on top of the same infrastructure, creating a competitive ecosystem without fragmenting the user experience. Payments are free or low-cost, settled in real time, and available 24/7, even on holidays.

Adoption has been staggering. UPI now manages billions of transactions monthly and reaches deep into rural areas where cash once dominated. It supports not just peer-to-peer transfers but merchant payments, bill payments, recurring mandates, and even microloans. It's also being extended internationally, with cross-border pilots linking it to systems in Singapore, the UAE, and beyond.

UPI isn't just a rail; it's a public utility with private-sector participation. It demonstrates how policy, infrastructure, and competition can align to build a real-time payment ecosystem that is fast, inclusive, and scalable.

SEPA (Single Euro Payments Area) – Europe

SEPA is the framework that enables fast, standardized euro payments across Europe. Developed by the European Payments Council and supported by the European Central Bank, SEPA was designed to simplify and unify the region's fragmented bank transfer systems. It allows individuals, businesses, and governments to send and receive payments in euros across participating countries as easily as they would domestically.

SEPA encompasses more than 30 countries, including all EU member states and several others that use the euro or align with EU financial standards. It supports both credit transfers and direct debits, with harmonized formats, settlement rules, and identifiers (like the IBAN and BIC). This interoperability has been essential for enabling cross-border commerce within the EU.

The SEPA Credit Transfer scheme typically settles payments within one business day. However, SEPA Instant, introduced more recently, enables near-instant settlement, 24/7, up to a defined euro amount (currently €100,000 in many regions). Not all banks have adopted SEPA Instant yet, but its footprint is growing quickly, especially among fintechs and platforms serving pan-European users.

SEPA's strength lies in its consistency. Whether you're paying a vendor in Berlin or reimbursing a contractor in Lisbon, the payment process is the same. This simplicity has helped reduce costs and friction for European businesses, and it supports the EU's broader push for financial integration.

However, SEPA is limited to euro-denominated payments, making it less useful for companies dealing in multi-currency flows or serving customers outside Europe. Still, within its domain, SEPA remains the gold standard for efficient, bank-based payments across borders.

INTERAC – Canada

INTERAC is Canada's dominant domestic payment network, known for powering real-time debit transactions and peer-to-peer money transfers across the country. While not a real-time payment rail in the strictest technical sense, INTERAC has long offered near-instant money movement for consumers and small businesses, particularly through its popular

INTERAC e-Transfer service.

INTERAC operates as a network connecting nearly all Canadian banks and credit unions. It supports everyday debit transactions at the point of sale, online purchases, and direct transfers between accounts via email or mobile number. For Canadian consumers, sending money via INTERAC e-Transfer is as common as writing a check once was, only faster and far more convenient.

Most e-Transfers are settled within minutes and include instant notification to recipients. The system operates extended hours, although it is not technically 24/7. Although it lacks the complete finality of a proper real-time gross settlement system, it has become fast and reliable enough to feel real-time to end users.

INTERAC is also evolving. It has added features like Autodeposit, which allows funds to be accepted without manual confirmation, and Request Money, enabling recipients to initiate payment flows. Additionally, Canada is in the process of rolling out the Real-Time Rail (RTR) under Payments Canada, a new infrastructure designed to complement and eventually extend what INTERAC started.

For now, INTERAC remains Canada's go-to platform for domestic transfers. It's trusted, widely integrated, and user-friendly, a strong example of how a country can build confidence in electronic payments without sacrificing reliability or scale.

NPP (New Payments Platform) – Australia

Australia's New Payments Platform, or NPP, is the country's real-time payment system designed to support fast, flexible, and data-rich transactions around the clock. Launched in 2018 through a collaboration between the Reserve Bank of Australia and key financial institutions, NPP enables individuals and businesses to send payments instantly between participating banks, with funds clearing and settling in real time.

One of NPP's standout features is the PayID system, which allows users to link their bank accounts to easy-to-remember identifiers, such as phone numbers, email addresses, or business ABNs, instead of relying on complex account and BSB numbers. This makes payments not only faster, but also simpler and less error prone.

In addition to speed and convenience, NPP also supports rich data messaging, allowing for up to 280 characters of payment information. This makes it worthwhile for business invoicing, payroll, and automated reconciliation. The system is also extensible, enabling overlays such as Osko, a consumer-facing brand that most Australians associate with real-time transfers, and government services like instant tax refunds or crisis payments.

Participation among banks has grown steadily, and NPP has become the new normal for peer-to-peer transfers and increasingly for B2B and government disbursements. While adoption in some sectors has lagged, regulatory pressure and market demand are accelerating its integration across industries.

The NPP reflects Australia's commitment to real-time, data-rich, interoperable payments, a platform designed not just for speed, but for innovation.

PayNow – Singapore

PayNow is Singapore's real-time payment system for individuals and businesses, built to enable fast, secure transfers using mobile numbers, national ID numbers, or corporate registration IDs as simple proxies for bank account details. Launched in 2017 by the Association of Banks in Singapore and the Monetary Authority of Singapore, PayNow has quickly become a staple of the country's digital economy.

What makes PayNow particularly elegant is its seamless integration across participating banks and digital wallets. Users can send money instantly 24/7, across banks and platforms, with no need to enter or know account numbers. The system supports peer-to-peer transfers, merchant payments, bill splitting, and even QR code–based point-of-sale transactions, all with real-time confirmation and no transaction fees for consumers.

PayNow is also tightly linked with FAST (Fast and Secure Transfers), the underlying infrastructure that processes the actual fund movements. The combination of PayNow's user interface and FAST's technical backbone allows Singaporeans to experience frictionless payments across a wide range of use cases, from hawker stalls to corporate payouts.

The system has seen widespread adoption among individuals, small businesses, and government agencies. It's also expanding cross-border functionality, with bilateral real-time payment corridors already established between Singapore and countries like Thailand and India.

In a city-state known for financial innovation and public-private collaboration, PayNow exemplifies how a well-designed payment overlay can dramatically simplify and accelerate how money moves, without compromising security or control.

SWIFT – Global

SWIFT, short for the Society for Worldwide Interbank Financial Telecommunication, is not a payment rail in the traditional sense; it doesn't move money directly, but it underpins much of the global financial system by providing the secure messaging infrastructure banks use to exchange payment instructions.

Founded in the 1970s and headquartered in Belgium, SWIFT connects more than 11,000 financial institutions across over 200 countries. It enables banks to coordinate cross-border transactions by standardizing how payment details are formatted, validated, and routed. Whether it's a USD wire to a U.S. bank, a euro transfers within the EU, or a multi-currency settlement between institutions in Asia and Africa, SWIFT is often the common language behind the scenes.

When someone sends an international wire, the actual funds may travel over domestic rails like Fedwire, CHIPS, or RTGS systems, but the SWIFT message is what triggers and coordinates the movement. It contains information about the sender, recipient, amount, currency, and purpose, and relies on SWIFT codes (BICs) to identify financial institutions.

Historically, SWIFT messages were tied to correspondent banking, a slower and more opaque system. But in recent years, SWIFT has evolved. It now supports richer data standards (like ISO 20022), improved tracking via SWIFT GPI (Global Payments Innovation), and initiatives to shorten delivery windows from days to minutes. Still, fees can be high, and intermediaries may take cuts or introduce delays.

While newer cross-border alternatives are emerging, including blockchain-based networks and real-time linkages, SWIFT remains the backbone of global interbank communication, particularly for high-value and regulated transactions.

CHAPS – United Kingdom

CHAPS (Clearing House Automated Payment System) is the UK's high-value, same-day settlement system operated by the Bank of England. It's designed for transactions where speed, certainty, and finality are non-negotiable, most often in wholesale banking, large corporate transfers, or property purchases.

Launched in 1984, CHAPS was one of the world's earliest real-time gross settlement (RTGS) systems. Payments sent via CHAPS are settled individually and irrevocably, with no batching or netting. Once a transaction is processed, the funds are final. There's no going back.

CHAPS is primarily used by financial institutions, law firms, and businesses needing to move large sums, often millions or tens of millions of pounds, quickly and with assurance. It's also used for critical infrastructure settlement and government transactions. Unlike retail systems like Faster Payments, CHAPS don't have a cap on payment size and doesn't run 24/7, but it operates during extended business hours with extremely high reliability.

Because it's a central bank–run system, CHAPS carries the full credibility and settlement security of the Bank of England. Over the years, its operational framework has evolved, aligning with ISO 20022 messaging standards and participating in broader UK payments modernization initiatives.

While it's invisible to most consumers, CHAPS plays an essential role in keeping the UK's financial system running smoothly, particularly where timing, trust, and transaction size demand the highest possible standards.

Summary: Global Payment Systems at a Glance

The global payment landscape is a mosaic of rails, some old, some new, each designed to meet different needs. Some systems prioritize scale and security over speed; others are built for instant gratification but may struggle with cross-border complexity or value limits. Understanding how these systems compare helps platforms, banks, and regulators choose the right tool for the right moment.

Here's how they stack up:

Speed and Settlement Finality

The speed at which a payment system settles transactions, and whether that settlement is final and irrevocable, is a defining characteristic of any rail. At the fast end of the spectrum, real-time payment systems like RTP (US), FedNow, PIX (Brazil), UPI (India), NPP (Australia), PayNow (Singapore), and Faster Payments (UK) enable money to move instantly. These platforms operate 24/7, providing both immediate confirmation and finality, making them ideal for time-sensitive consumer payments, disbursements, and business flows.

In contrast, high-value real-time gross settlement (RTGS) systems such as Fedwire (US), CHAPS (UK), and CHIPS (US) also offer settlement finality, but typically do so only during designated business hours. These systems prioritize reliability and liquidity control, catering to institutional users who need to move large sums securely and with certainty, even if not instantaneously.

Legacy systems like ACH in the U.S. and SEPA Credit Transfers in Europe follow a batch-processing model. Payments are grouped and cleared in cycles, often introducing a delay of one to two business days. While newer enhancements like Same-Day ACH and SEPA Instant aim to bridge the gap, their coverage is still evolving, and many payments continue to follow slower settlement paths.

SWIFT stands apart as a messaging network rather than a payment rail. The speed of a SWIFT-enabled transaction depends on the underlying systems used for settlement. Historically, this could involve multi-day delays, especially with correspondent banking. However, innovations like SWIFT GPI (Global Payments Innovation) have significantly improved both speed and transparency, enabling many transactions to be tracked and settled within the same day.

Access and User Experience

The accessibility of a payment system, both in terms of who can use it and how easily, plays a critical role in driving adoption and shaping user behavior. Systems like UPI in India, PIX in Brazil, and PayNow in Singapore were designed from the ground up with end users in mind. These platforms emphasize simplicity, allowing people to send money using only a mobile number, national ID, or QR code. Their interfaces are intuitive, often embedded in banking apps or widely used third-party platforms, making digital payments feel effortless for both consumers and small businesses.

In mature economies like the UK and Canada, systems such as Faster Payments and INTERAC e-Transfer offer a similar level of usability. While originally bank-driven, these systems have evolved to support features like auto-deposit, request-for-payment, and mobile integration, creating a consumer experience that feels fast, familiar, and increasingly seamless.

At the other end of the spectrum are high-value systems like Fedwire (US), CHAPS (UK), and CHIPS (US), which are not designed for public use. These platforms serve banks, corporations, and institutional players managing large-sum or high-stakes transactions. Their interfaces are rarely consumer-facing and often require secure, enterprise-grade integrations and formal banking relationships.

SWIFT also occupies a behind-the-scenes role in the user experience. As a messaging layer, it facilitates bank-to-bank communication for cross-border transfers, but the end user may never interact with it directly. That said, initiatives like SWIFT GPI have improved visibility and tracking for users, giving them real-time status updates and estimated arrival times for international payments, a significant shift from the historical opacity of global wires.

Overall, user experience varies widely by system. Consumer-first platforms prioritize ease of use, speed, and mobile accessibility. Institutional systems focus on security, precision, and compliance. The gap between these approaches is narrowing as user expectations rise, even in traditionally closed, high-value environments.

Scope: Domestic vs. Cross-Border

While many payment systems are optimized for domestic use, a growing number are extending their reach across borders, though the landscape remains fragmented. Domestic rails like ACH, FedNow, RTP, CHAPS, Faster Payments, and INTERAC are designed to move money efficiently within national boundaries. They are tightly integrated with local banking infrastructure, regulatory frameworks, and currency standards, which makes them fast and reliable for internal transfers but inherently limited for international payments.

For cross-border transactions, SWIFT remains the central artery. It doesn't move money itself, but instead coordinates the messaging between financial institutions, enabling funds to be routed through correspondent banks across different countries and currencies. Despite its longstanding dominance, SWIFT has faced growing criticism for its opacity and delays. In response, the SWIFT gpi initiative has added much-needed transparency and speed, allowing payments to be tracked and settled more efficiently, sometimes within hours, rather than days.

Some domestic systems are now pushing beyond their original borders. UPI in India and PayNow in Singapore, for example, have established bilateral corridors that enable real-time payments between users in different countries. These cross-border linkages are still in early stages. Still, they represent a significant shift, one where domestic systems are beginning to interoperate in ways that bypass traditional correspondent banking networks.

SEPA, while technically domestic to the Eurozone, is itself a multinational system. It enables cross-border payments across more than 30 European countries with the same ease as domestic transfers, though only for euro-denominated transactions. This regional model offers a glimpse into what broader cross-border harmonization could look like.

In short, while domestic systems offer speed and consistency within borders, actual cross-border efficiency still depends on a patchwork of integrations, standards, and interbank agreements. The challenge ahead is turning that patchwork into something closer to a seamless global network.

Takeaway: No single system dominates globally. Cross-border payments remain fragmented, though integration efforts are accelerating.

Governance and Infrastructure Design

The governance behind a payment system often shapes how it evolves, who can access it, and how quickly it can respond to innovation or regulatory shifts. Systems operated by central banks, such as FedNow in the U.S., PIX in Brazil, and UPI in India, are typically built with public policy goals in mind. These platforms focus on broad accessibility, financial inclusion, and interoperability, treating payment infrastructure as a public good rather than a commercial product.

Privately operated systems, such as RTP and CHIPS (both run by The Clearing House in the U.S.), emphasize speed, resilience, and functionality, but access and development are often driven by the interests of their bank shareholders. These systems are robust and stable but may be slower to extend access to smaller institutions or fintechs unless required by regulation.

Cooperative frameworks like SWIFT and SEPA represent a middle ground. They're not-for-profit and designed to serve large networks of banks, but the need for multilateral consensus sometimes constrains their ability to innovate quickly. Still, they offer a degree of standardization and global reach that's difficult for smaller or newer systems to replicate.

Governance also influences technology choices. For example, ISO 20022, a global messaging standard, is being adopted by many newer systems and retrofitted into legacy ones like Fedwire, SWIFT, and CHAPS to enable richer, more structured payment data. Meanwhile, open-access initiatives and API-driven infrastructure are becoming the norm for consumer-facing platforms.

Ultimately, the rules, priorities, and stakeholders behind a payment rail shape how inclusive, agile, and future proof it becomes. A rail's technology may be real-time, but if its governance is slow or exclusive, its full potential can remain out of reach.

Choosing the Right Rail

There is no single "best" payment system; instead, the best fit varies by specific use case, geography, and business model. Real-time consumer payments, for example, are best served by platforms like UPI in India, PIX in Brazil, or PayNow in Singapore. These systems prioritize speed, ease of use, and accessibility, making them ideal for everyday transactions and digital commerce.

For high-value institutional transfers where timing and settlement finality are non-negotiable, systems like Fedwire, CHAPS, and CHIPS remain essential. They offer immediate or same-day settlement with robust risk controls, serving as the backbone for corporate, interbank, and securities-related flows.

When it comes to cross-border movement, SWIFT still plays a central role. Its messaging infrastructure underpins most international transactions, particularly those involving multiple currencies or complex regulatory environments. However, pressure for modernization is growing, and newer models are beginning to chip away at its dominance, often by improving transparency, speed, and cost.

As real-time, data-rich systems continue to expand and interoperability improves across borders and platforms, the boundaries between domestic and international payments, and between retail and institutional use cases, are starting to blur. The future of payments is unlikely to be defined by any one rail. Instead, it will be shaped by a network of networks: interlinked, API-driven, standardized, and anchored in trust.

The Rise of Real-Time Payment Rails

As digital commerce accelerates and customer expectations evolve, the need for instant, reliable, and transparent payments has never been greater. Legacy payment systems, with their batch-based architecture and delayed settlement, were never designed for a world that operates 24/7, across borders and platforms. Enter real-time payment rails, modern infrastructure built from the ground up to move money immediately, with confirmation, finality, and flexibility.

Unlike legacy rails that settle hours or even days after a transaction is initiated, real-time rails settle in seconds, with irrevocable confirmation and integrated messaging. These systems are transforming how individuals, businesses, and even governments move funds, driving new use cases and changing the very expectations around what a payment should feel like.

Why Real-Time Rails Matter Now

Real-time payments aren't just faster. They're fundamentally different ways of thinking about money movement. They unlock business models, such as just-in-time payroll, instant refunds, or usage-based billing, which were previously impossible with traditional rails. They also improve user trust, reduce working capital strain, and lower fraud by narrowing the window for reversal or account compromise.

And perhaps most importantly, they signal a shift in control: from banks to platforms, from static settlement cycles to dynamic flows, and from days to seconds.

Real-time rails are no longer optional. They are becoming the default infrastructure for the digital economy.

Evolving Risk Exposure in a Decentralized Model

The payments ecosystem is no longer built around a single bank, processor, or platform. It's evolved into a decentralized, multi-layered web of institutions, APIs, infrastructure providers, and embedded services, all of which must interact seamlessly to move money. This decentralization has enabled innovation, flexibility, and reach. But it has also significantly expanded the risk surface.

In legacy systems, payment functions were centralized. One institution, typically a large bank, issued cards, held deposits, processed transactions, and maintained oversight. Today, a single transaction might involve a fintech front-end, a Banking-as-a-Service provider, a third-party fraud vendor, a sponsor bank, and a real-time payment rail, all stitched together in milliseconds.

Each of these layers introduces new potential points of failure, including compliance gaps, API outages, data mismatches, inconsistent fraud logic, and regulatory misalignment. When these risks are not managed holistically, they don't just affect one layer; they cascade across the stack.

A core challenge in decentralized models is diffused accountability. When something goes wrong, such as a breach, an unauthorized transaction, or a regulatory violation, it's often unclear who is responsible. Was it the front-end app? The infrastructure partner? The sponsor bank? This ambiguity complicates everything from incident response to legal liability.

Another consequence of decentralization is the rise of interdependency risk. Payment platforms increasingly rely on a few key third parties for critical functions: cloud services, identity verification, fraud scoring, ledgering, and money movement. If any of these providers fail, due to outages, cyberattacks, regulatory action, or insolvency, the downstream consequences can be severe. Entire platforms have had to pause operations after losing access to a core banking or compliance partner.

And then there's risk velocity. In decentralized systems operating on real-time rails, threats spread fast. A bad actor exploiting an onboarding flaw can launch dozens of synthetic identities across a platform in minutes. A fraud pattern that once took days to evolve can now execute in seconds. Traditional risk tools, batch monitoring, end-of-day reviews, and quarterly audits are insufficient. What's needed is real-time detection, layered defenses, and continuous learning systems.

Finally, decentralization has made regulatory complexity the norm. Fintechs and PSPs may operate across multiple jurisdictions, each with different expectations for KYC, data retention, fraud reporting, and consumer protection. Even if the company is technically unregulated in one market, its partners may be, creating compliance obligations by proxy.

In this new model, risk doesn't follow neat lines. It moves laterally, hides in integrations, and accelerates with scale. The only way to manage it effectively is to embed risk awareness into every decision layer, product, engineering, compliance, customer experience, and vendor management.

Because in a decentralized world, there is no single point of failure, but there are thousands of potential points of exposure.

Bottom Line: Legacy rails still matter, and likely will for years. But the momentum is clear: the future is instant. In today's instant world, risk must be managed at the speed of the transaction.

Key Regulations Shaping Risk Management in Payments

In the modern payments' ecosystem, regulation isn't a back-office burden; it's a strategic layer of defense, defining how financial institutions operate, how innovation is shaped, and where risk boundaries are drawn. Regulatory frameworks do more than enforce minimum standards; they set the tone for everything from system architecture and onboarding flows to data retention and fraud response.

Around the world, regulators have introduced region-specific and global standards that influence how payment companies approach security, transparency, and trust. Understanding these regulatory foundations isn't optional; it's essential for anyone building or managing a payments business.

PSD2: Unlocking Innovation, and Risk, Through Open Banking

In the European Union, the revised Payment Services Directive (PSD2) marked a turning point in payments regulation. Designed to promote innovation and competition, PSD2 requires banks to open their infrastructure and customer account data to licensed third-party providers via APIs, a concept known as open banking.

While this mandate has driven a wave of fintech development, it has also introduced new dimensions of risk. Strong Customer Authentication (SCA), another key requirement under PSD2, was introduced to reduce fraud. But if implemented poorly, SCA can degrade the user experience and increase cart abandonment in e-commerce flows.

For payment providers, PSD2 means more than just regulatory paperwork. It demands real-time monitoring of third-party activity, robust consent management, and a proactive approach to third-party risk, because when infrastructure is opened, so are the doors to new vulnerabilities.

PCI DSS: The Global Gold Standard for Card Data Security

Enforced globally by the major card networks, the Payment Card Industry Data Security Standard (PCI DSS) governs how cardholder data is stored, transmitted, and processed. At its core, PCI DSS is a technical and operational blueprint for protecting payment data, one that continues to evolve as threats and attack surfaces change.

For payment processors, acquirers, and merchants, non-compliance with PCI DSS can be costly: fines, increased interchange fees, and even the loss of card-processing privileges. Beyond the regulatory exposure, PCI requirements are often central in post-breach forensic investigations, where companies must prove that data protection protocols were in place and enforced.

Compliance demands include robust encryption, access control, vulnerability patching, file integrity monitoring, and audit logging, all of which must be maintained continuously, not just annually.

AML and KYC: The Regulatory Front Lines of Financial Crime Prevention

Anti-Money Laundering (AML) laws, often based on FATF (Financial Action Task Force) guidance, are now enforced in nearly every market. These regulations require payment companies to identify customers, monitor transactions for suspicious patterns, and report anomalies to relevant authorities.

Closely tied to AML is KYC (Know Your Customer), the process of verifying customer identities before enabling access to financial products. Weak or outdated KYC procedures remain one of the most exploited entry points for fraudsters, particularly in digital-first or cross-border environments.

Together, AML and KYC frameworks force payment companies to invest in automated identity verification, behavioral analytics, and machine learning–driven anomaly detection. Failures are costly, not just financially, but reputationally. Regulatory fines for inadequate due diligence or reporting failures are among the most common enforcement actions in the payments space.

Yet these controls must be carefully balanced. Too much friction in the KYC process leads to drop-offs, too little invites fraud. The art of compliance in this space lies in building systems that are both secure and seamless.

GDPR: Data Privacy as a Risk Imperative

In the European Union, the General Data Protection Regulation (GDPR) has redefined how payment platforms manage personal data. Far from a niche IT concern, GDPR sits at the heart of operational risk. Companies must now justify every data point collected, ensure secure storage, and provide mechanisms for users to manage or delete their information.

For payments companies, which deal in behavioral data, transactional metadata, and often biometric identifiers, GDPR presents both a challenge and a warning. A single breach can trigger fines up to 4% of global annual revenue, alongside lasting damage to brand trust.

Additionally, GDPR impacts how fraud data, customer profiling, and analytics logs are used, requiring explicit consent, purpose limitation, and strict access control. The standard forces organizations to treat user data not just as an asset, but as a regulated liability.

U.S. Frameworks: A Patchwork with Teeth

In the United States, there is no single unified payments regulator, but several key laws define the risk landscape:

The Bank Secrecy Act (BSA) forms the foundation of AML obligations, requiring institutions to file Suspicious Activity Reports (SARs) and maintain detailed records.

OFAC (Office of Foreign Assets Control) mandates real-time sanction screening, blocking transactions from or to blocked entities or jurisdictions.

The Dodd-Frank Act, and more specifically the Consumer Financial Protection Bureau (CFPB), has placed pressure on payment companies to improve transparency around fees, disclosures, and dispute handling, making consumer fairness a top operational risk concern.

While less centralized than the EU model, U.S. enforcement actions are often high-profile and severe, especially when it comes to AML failures, mismanagement of consumer complaints, or deceptive practices.

Other Critical Standards and Frameworks

Several technical and international frameworks also shape how payment companies manage risk:

ISO 20022: A global messaging standard that enhances interoperability, metadata transmission, and reconciliation, increasingly crucial for real-time and cross-border transactions.

EMV (Europay, Mastercard, Visa): The global chip card standard that significantly reduced card-present fraud by replacing magnetic stripes with encrypted chips.

Basel III: Though primarily aimed at banking institutions, its focus on capital adequacy and liquidity management has cascading effects on regulated payment institutions, especially those offering stored value, lending, or reserve-backed services.

Regulation as a Strategic Control Layer

These frameworks are not isolated silos; they interlock and overlap, collectively defining what "good risk management" looks like in payments. Companies that treat regulation reactively, as a hurdle to clear, often find themselves in the crosshairs of regulators, card networks, or public opinion.

The most resilient payment organizations recognize regulation as a strategic advantage. They build systems that are not just compliant, but transparent, flexible, and audit ready. Because in today's global ecosystem, regulatory readiness isn't a legal checkbox, it's a signal of trustworthiness, maturity, and long-term viability.

Regulatory Complexity Is Risk Complexity

As payment platforms grow across borders, so too does their exposure to a sprawling, often conflicting patchwork of regulatory regimes. What protects consumers and markets in one district may contradict or exceed expectations in another. The result is a landscape where compliance becomes not just a legal challenge, but a strategic risk.

Operating in multiple countries means navigating overlapping data privacy rules, divergent KYC thresholds, competing definitions of beneficial ownership, and inconsistent reporting obligations. Even well-intentioned companies can fall out of step with local regulations, not because of misconduct, but because scale outpaces structure.

This introduces several real-world threats:

Regulatory arbitrage occurs when companies take advantage of inconsistencies or gaps between different regulatory frameworks, often unintentionally, to operate in ways that may not align with the spirit of the law. This can happen, for example, when a business launches in multiple jurisdictions without fully understanding how local rules differ, leading to compliance blind spots.

Compliance fatigue sets in when an organization's growth outpaces the ability of its internal compliance teams to keep up. As products expand, new markets open, and regulations evolve, teams can become overwhelmed, increasing the risk of missed obligations, superficial reviews, or outdated policies.

Enforcement risk arises when regulators identify non-compliance and choose to act, whether through fines, audits, restrictions, or public censure. This risk increases significantly when compliance gaps are repeated, delayed, or poorly documented, even if the intent was not malicious.

The solution isn't just hiring more lawyers. It's embedding regulatory literacy into product development, engineering, customer experience, and vendor management, turning compliance from a function into a mindset. The companies that do this well don't just survive, they win trust, scale more predictably, and stay ahead of costly surprises.

Evolving Risk Exposure in a Decentralized Model

The decentralization of payments, with APIs, BaaS providers, PSPs, and fintech wrappers, has made transactions faster and more modular. But it has also introduced diffused responsibility, more failure points, and accelerated risk velocity.

When responsibility is shared across vendors and partners, the ability to manage risk depends on one thing: visibility. Who controls what? Who detects what? Who acts when something goes wrong?

Without clear answers, risk doesn't just slip through cracks; it travels through them.

As platforms decentralize further, their resilience will depend not on removing complexity, but on managing it transparently and proactively. That requires tighter vendor oversight, real-time monitoring, and collaborative accountability across the stack.

Chapter Summary: The Shape of Modern Payments

The payments ecosystem has never been more dynamic or more complex. What was once a linear process between banks is now a distributed, high-velocity network of issuers, acquirers, PSPs, ISOs, fintechs, and third-party providers, all interacting across legacy and real-time rails. Each player adds value, but also introduces new forms of risk: operational, reputational, financial, and structural.

Speed, scale, and seamless user experiences have become the standard, but they come at a cost. Risk no longer hides in obvious places. It travels through code, vendors, integrations, and behaviors. And with decentralization, there is no longer a single chokepoint where everything can be observed and controlled. Instead, risk management must be distributed, proactive, and deeply embedded into every layer of operations and infrastructure.

As we move forward, understanding the nature and categories of these risks becomes essential, not just for preventing fraud or meeting compliance, but for building a payments business that can endure.

That's where we turn next: breaking down the most critical types of risk facing modern payment providers, and how to detect, categorize, and respond to them in real time.

Chapter 2: Categories of Risk in Payments

In the fast-moving world of payments, risk is everywhere, but it's not all the same. Some risks are financial, directly tied to fraud, credit exposure, or liquidity gaps. Others are operational, hidden in systems, vendors, or human error. Then there are regulatory and reputational risks, slow-burning, long-tailed, but equally capable of bringing down platforms if left unchecked.

To manage risk effectively, payment organizations must first understand their operational environment. This involves categorizing risk, identifying its occurrence, evolution, and ownership. A chargeback isn't just a loss; it's a potential symptom of onboarding gaps, policy weaknesses, or abusive behavior patterns. A failed KYC check isn't just a compliance issue; it's a point of exposure that could open the door to laundering, synthetic identity fraud, or regulatory fines.

Unlike traditional financial institutions, modern payments companies often operate at the edge of speed, scale, and innovation. This makes them especially vulnerable to interconnected risks, where a failure in one domain (like customer verification) rapidly cascades into another (like unauthorized transactions or regulator attention).

In this chapter, we'll explore the major categories of risk payment providers must face:

➤ Financial Risk, credit exposure, liquidity shortfalls, and fraud losses

➤ Operational Risk, outages, vendor failures, process gaps, and human error

➤ Fraud and Cyber Risk, synthetic identities, account takeover, and data breaches.

➤ Regulatory and Compliance Risk, failing to meet standards for AML, KYC, sanctions, and reporting.

➤ Reputational Risk, public trust, media fallout, and ecosystem-wide damage

Each of these categories is distinct, but they're rarely isolated. The most resilient payment organizations don't treat them as checkboxes. They treat them as signals, linked in a chain that's only as strong as its weakest node.

Let's start where risk is most tangible: money lost, money frozen, or money moved in ways it shouldn't be.

Financial Risk

At the heart of every payments business lies a simple promise: that money will move quickly, securely, and predictably. But that promise depends on a delicate balance of trust, timing, and capital. When that balance is disrupted by bad actors, market volatility, or operational shortfalls, financial risk becomes real.

In the payments industry, financial risk typically takes two primary forms: credit risk and liquidity risk. While they're often related, they represent distinct challenges that require different strategies to manage.

Credit Risk: When Counterparties Fail

Credit risk arises when a participant in the payment flow, a merchant, consumer, or financial partner, is unable or unwilling to meet their financial obligations. In traditional banking, this often looks like a loan default. In payments, it's more often tied to merchant failure, chargeback liability, or settlement default.

For example, consider a PSP that processes $1 million in card transactions for a merchant over a week. If the merchant goes out of business before fulfilling customer orders, cardholders may initiate chargebacks. The card networks will claw back the funds, but the merchant is gone. Now the PSP is on the hook. That's credit risk.

It's also present when working with platform clients, resellers, or white-label partners. A poorly capitalized ISO may fail to pay its residual fees. A cross-border merchant might delay refund payouts due to FX volatility. A sudden spike in refunds may exceed the merchant's reserve, leaving the PSP exposed.

To manage credit risk, payment companies employ a range of tools designed to limit exposure when a merchant or counterparty cannot fulfill their financial obligations. These mechanisms are fundamental in environments were chargebacks, refunds, or sudden business failures could result in unrecoverable losses. The most common credit risk management techniques include:

Rolling reserves involve withholding a fixed percentage of a merchant's incoming funds for a predetermined period, typically 30, 60, or 90 days. This reserve acts as a buffer to cover potential chargebacks, disputes, or unexpected liabilities. By releasing the withheld funds only after the risk window has passed, the platform ensures it has capital on hand to absorb any downstream exposure.

Delayed settlements postpone the payout of funds to a merchant after a transaction is processed. Rather than settling funds instantly or within one day, payment processors may delay disbursement by several days to allow time for fraud checks, chargeback monitoring, or fulfillment verification. This time buffer helps reduce the risk of releasing funds to merchants who may later be found to have acted fraudulently or gone out of business.

Transaction limits and velocity thresholds set caps on the dollar value or volume of transactions a merchant can process within a given time limit, such as per day, week, or month. These limits help prevent a sudden spike in activity that could indicate fraud, money laundering, or operational instability. Velocity thresholds also allow platforms to gradually increase trust as a merchant's behavior proves consistent and low risk over time.

Tiered risk scoring, applied both during onboarding and throughout a merchant's lifecycle, helps classify merchants based on their industry, transaction patterns, history, and behavioral data. Higher-risk merchants, such as those in subscription billing, travel, or digital goods, may face stricter controls, while lower-risk merchants may qualify for faster settlement or lower reserve requirements. Ongoing monitoring ensures that merchants can be re-scored dynamically as their behavior changes.

These tools are often used in combination, creating a layered approach that balances merchant experience with platform protection. When implemented thoughtfully, they allow payment providers to support a wide range of businesses while minimizing the risk of financial loss.

None of these eliminates the risk, but they absorb the shock and give the platform time to respond.

Liquidity Risk: When Cash Isn't Where You Need It

Liquidity risk is more subtle, but just as dangerous. It occurs when an organization can't access funds fast enough to meet its obligations, even if it's technically solvent. In a real-time payment environment, this can happen quickly.

Imagine a PSP supporting instant payouts to gig workers. If those payouts are pre-funded and user activity spikes, the platform may need to front millions of dollars before receiving settlement from acquiring banks. If the treasury team isn't prepared, or if a bank experiences a delay, the company might fail to meet its obligations, triggering operational breakdowns and reputational damage.

Liquidity risk is also amplified in cross-border transactions, where currency exchange delays, capital controls, or bank holidays can freeze flows. Even temporary disruptions can harm user trust, especially in markets where payments are expected in seconds, not days.

Effective liquidity management is essential for any payments business, particularly those operating in real-time environments or under tight capital constraints. It ensures that funds are available exactly when needed to fulfill customer payouts, settle with partners, or meet regulatory obligations without tying up unnecessary working capital. To achieve this, leading platforms implement several key practices:

Intraday cash forecasting and treasury dashboards provide real-time visibility into cash movements across accounts, currencies, and partners. By modeling expected inflows and outflows throughout the day, treasury teams can anticipate shortfalls or surpluses and respond accordingly. Modern dashboards consolidate balances, pending settlements, and transaction pipelines into a single view, enabling faster, more informed decisions and tighter operational control.

Settlement schedule optimization involves aligning payout timing with known funding inflows and outflows. Rather than treating settlement as a static process, savvy platforms adjust timing based on factors like transaction volume, time zones, and banking cutoffs. This helps minimize the risk of overdrafts, liquidity bottlenecks, or idle capital trapped in transit.

Pre-funding strategies and credit lines provide a financial cushion for high-volume or high-velocity payment flows. In cases where customer expectations or operational design require payouts before funds are received (such as instant wage disbursements or just-in-time supplier payments), platforms may pre-fund settlement accounts or tap into revolving credit facilities. These tools bridge timing gaps and ensure business continuity, even when upstream delays occur.

Multiple banking relationships serve as both a diversification strategy and a resilience mechanism. By maintaining accounts with more than one financial institution, platforms can spread counterparty exposure, mitigate the risk of service interruptions, and optimize for geographic or currency-specific needs. This is especially critical in regions where local banks may be subject to outages, regulatory freezes, or capital controls.

For many modern payment companies, especially those operating in emerging markets or with razor-thin margins, liquidity management is not just a finance function. It is core infrastructure. Without it, even the most advanced payment architecture can halt, not because of fraud or regulatory issues, but because the right funds weren't in the right place at the right time.

The Interplay of Credit and Liquidity

These two risk categories are deeply interwoven. A sudden spike in merchant defaults (credit risk) can deplete cash reserves and trigger liquidity shortfalls. Conversely, liquidity constraints may force delayed payments or missed obligations, damaging reputation and creating regulatory risk. Left unmanaged, financial risk can ripple through the entire ecosystem, affecting not just a single player but their networks, customers, and counterparties.

For this reason, financial risk management in payments is not just about solvency; it's about fluidity, predictability, and trust. And in an industry where velocity is everything, the ability to manage financial exposure in real time is no longer optional; it's mission critical.

Financial risk is immediate. It shows up in balances, disputes, frozen payouts, and loss reports. But it's also systemic, tied to how platforms structure their revenue, handle reserves, and model risk across merchant portfolios. It's where trust meets capital.

Next, we explore the risk that often triggers financial loss: operational risk, when processes, systems, or people fail.

Operational Risk

In payments, money may move at the speed of code, but it still depends on people, systems, and processes that are anything but perfect. Operational risk is the category that captures all the way a payment platform can falter from within outages, failed processes, human error, vendor missteps, or even configuration mistakes.

What makes operational risk uniquely dangerous is that it's often invisible until it breaks something. A misconfigured API call may allow duplicate transactions. A missed alert in the fraud system could let a criminal ring slip through onboarding. An incorrectly formatted payment file might result in delayed settlement to thousands of merchants. These aren't always dramatic failures, but they compound over time, quietly draining confidence, capital, and compliance.

System Failures and Downtime

Few things erode trust faster than a platform outage. Whether it's a gateway going offline, a cloud region failure, or a database timeout, technical disruptions have an immediate financial impact. Transactions are lost. Payouts are delayed. Merchants start looking for alternatives.

Payment systems operate under an expectation of continuous availability, especially with the rise of real-time settlement and global commerce. But the stack is complex: microservices, third-party dependencies, cloud infrastructure, message queues, databases, and edge networks. Each one introduces failure points. When something goes wrong, platforms must respond fast, not just to fix the issue, but to communicate clearly with affected stakeholders.

Vendor and Partner Dependencies

Modern payments are rarely managed in-house from end to end. PSPs, fintechs, and platforms rely on a network of external providers, including KYC vendors, compliance tools, acquiring banks, core processors, fraud engines, and payout aggregators. These integrations allow for speed and specialization, but they also shift operational risk beyond the organization's direct control.

If a KYC vendor experiences downtime, onboarding stops. If a bank API changes without notice, payouts may fail. If a fraudulent provider incorrectly flags legitimate transactions, conversion drops. In these cases, even if the platform isn't at fault, it bears the customer impact, and often the regulatory burden too.

Risk-aware companies treat vendors not as static plug-ins, but as dynamic extensions of their infrastructure.

That means formal due diligence, redundancy plans, performance SLAs, and real-time monitoring for vendor health.

Process Failures and Human Error

It's easy to focus on systems, but many operational failures originate with humans and workflows. A team member mislabels a merchant category. A payout file is uploaded to the wrong bank. A risk rule is deactivated during a deployment. These mistakes are usually unintentional, but they can lead to significant downstream consequences, from regulatory fines to reputational damage.

Managing operational risk is not just about fixing problems when they arise; it's about preventing them from escalating in the first place. In complex, high-volume payment environments, even a minor misconfiguration, missed handoff, or unauthorized change can have cascading consequences. To mitigate this, leading payment companies invest in several critical safeguards:

Process automation is one of the most effective ways to reduce human error. By eliminating manual steps in payment flows, reconciliation, reporting, or compliance checks, companies can significantly reduce the likelihood of mistakes resulting from fatigue, distraction, or inconsistency. Automation not only improves accuracy but also boosts speed and scalability, essential for teams managing thousands or millions of daily transactions.

Role-based access controls and structured change approval flows ensure that only the right people can perform sensitive actions, and only with the proper oversight. Whether it's adjusting a settlement file, modifying fraud rules, or deploying production code, platforms must enforce strict permissions and require documented approvals. These controls help prevent unauthorized changes, insider threats, or accidental missteps that could affect financial or operational integrity.

Runbooks and incident response playbooks provide a predefined roadmap for handling operational incidents. Rather than scrambling to respond in the heat of a system outage, data breach, or settlement failure, teams can follow documented steps, who to notify, what to assess, and how to communicate, reducing downtime and limiting damage. The best-run operations teams train against these scenarios regularly to stay sharp and responsive under pressure.

Postmortems and root cause analysis are essential for turning failures into lessons. After an incident, disciplined organizations conduct structured reviews to identify what went wrong, why it happened, and how similar issues can be prevented in the future. These reviews aren't about blame; they're about building institutional memory and continuously improving systems, processes, and culture.

No company can eliminate human error. But those who invest in automation, structure, and reflection create a culture of resilience. In these environments, minor missteps are caught before they grow into major failures, and when issues do arise, they're managed with speed, transparency, and clarity.

Operational risk isn't always headline-grabbing. It doesn't always result in fraud, lawsuits, or lost millions. But it is relentless, accumulative, and increasingly public. In the era of real-time, embedded payments, even short disruptions can destroy hard-earned user trust.

Next, we look at a category of risk that's both persistent and evolving fraud and cyber threats, where actors actively evaluate the defenses of your systems every day.

Fraud and Cyber Risk

Every payment platform is under attack, even if it doesn't know it yet. Fraudsters, social engineers, bots, and organized cybercriminals are constantly testing defenses, probing for weaknesses, and looking for the path of least resistance. Fraud and cyber risk are not occasional events. It's an ever-present background force, one that evolves just as fast as the systems trying to stop it.

Unlike credit or operational risk, which are often internal, fraud and cyber threats are adversarial. They're intentional, adaptive, and increasingly sophisticated. And in the digital age, they usually arrive disguised as legitimate users, transactions, or partners.

Fraud Tactics in Payments

Fraud in payments is not a single threat; it's a constantly evolving landscape of tactics, each with its signature patterns and motivations. As digital transactions grow more seamless, fraudsters have grown more creative, probing for weaknesses in onboarding flows, checkout systems, identity verification, and user behavior models. Some of the most common forms of payment fraud include:

Card testing is a tactic where fraudsters use stolen credit or debit card details to make small, low-risk purchases, often under the radar of fraud detection systems, to determine whether the card is still active. Once validated, the card may be used for larger, more damaging transactions elsewhere. These micro-transactions often hit donation sites, trial subscriptions, or e-commerce platforms with weak velocity checks.

Synthetic identity fraud involves the creation of entirely fake personas using a blend of real and fabricated information, for example, a real Social Security number paired with a false name and date of birth. Fraudsters use these identities to open accounts, build trust, and eventually cash out or launder funds. This type of fraud is challenging to detect because synthetic profiles can mimic legitimate users for months or even years before defaulting.

Account takeover (ATO) occurs when a fraudster gains unauthorized access to a user's account. This can be achieved through methods like phishing, credential stuffing (using leaked passwords from other sites), or SIM swapping, which intercepts two-factor authentication codes. Once inside, the attacker may change settings, drain funds, or make fraudulent purchases that appear authorized from the outside.

Friendly fraud occurs when a legitimate customer disputes a transaction, rather than a criminal outsider. Sometimes it's unintentional (a family member makes a purchase the cardholder doesn't recognize), but in many cases it's deliberate. Customers may falsely claim an item was never received or that they didn't authorize a charge, seeking a refund while keeping the goods or services.

Merchant fraud involves businesses that onboard with fraudulent intent. These merchants may process fake transactions, launder money through shell storefronts, or violate card network rules intentionally, for example, by misrepresenting business types or inflating sales to secure better terms. This type of fraud can expose payment providers to regulatory scrutiny, chargeback spikes, and reputational damage.

Each fraud tactic leaves a different footprint, in timing, behavior, volume, or device data, and each requires a tailored response. No single rule or system can catch them all. That's why modern fraud prevention relies on a layered approach: combining rule-based filters with machine learning models, behavioral analytics, and human review. The goal isn't just to block fraud, but to evolve with it, and to stay one step ahead of increasingly sophisticated threats.

Cyber Risk and Data Security

In the payments world, fraud rarely begins at the checkout screen. It often starts further upstream, with a breach of infrastructure, a compromised credential, or an overlooked system vulnerability. A single phishing email, an exposed API key, or an unpatched server can open the door for attackers to access sensitive data, manipulate transaction flows, or disrupt services entirely. Once inside, bad actors may exfiltrate cardholder data, alter routing rules, or escalate their access to shut down mission-critical systems.

Because of this, modern payment companies must adopt a zero-trust approach to security. Zero trust assumes that no system, device, or user, internal or external, should be trusted by default. Access must be verified continuously, and every layer of the stack must be protected independently.

End-to-end encryption is essential for protecting sensitive data, whether it's card details, personal identifiers, or settlement instructions. Encryption ensures that even if data is intercepted, it remains unintelligible without the appropriate keys, significantly reducing the risk of leakage during transit or at rest.

Multi-factor authentication (MFA) adds a critical layer of security to user access. By requiring a second form of verification, such as a one-time code, hardware token, or biometric check, MFA helps prevent unauthorized access even when login credentials are compromised.

Intrusion detection and anomaly alerting allow security teams to identify suspicious behavior in real time. Whether it's an unusual login pattern, a surge in traffic to a sensitive endpoint, or changes to transaction configurations, modern detection systems use rule sets and machine learning to flag emerging threats before they escalate.

Role-based access to production systems is another cornerstone of security hygiene. Employees and vendors should only be able to access the systems and data necessary for their specific role, nothing more. Limiting permissions in this way reduces the attack surface and helps contain damage if a user account is compromised.

Vendor security audits and penetration testing are essential for managing third-party risk. Most payment platforms rely on an ecosystem of external providers for KYC, cloud hosting, fraud tools, and more. Auditing those vendors, testing for vulnerabilities, and ensuring compliance with security standards like PCI DSS and SOC 2 is critical for maintaining a strong defense posture.

Cyber risk is no longer just an IT concern. It's a payment concern. A breach can compromise customer trust, regulatory standing, and operational continuity in a single stroke. As fraud becomes more sophisticated and infrastructure more interconnected, cybersecurity becomes inseparable from payment integrity, fraud defense, and long-term resilience.

Balancing Prevention with Experience

In the world of digital payments, fraud prevention is not just a technical problem; it's a user experience challenge and a business strategy decision. Every fraud control introduces friction, and every friction point risks turning away legitimate customers. Too many hurdles, like multi-step logins, declined transactions, or false-positive alerts, can frustrate users, increase abandonment, and damage brand trust. But remove those controls entirely, and a platform becomes an easy target for fraudsters and abuse.

The most mature organizations understand this tension and move beyond static, one-size-fits-all rules. Instead, they deploy dynamic systems that adapt to behavior and context, minimizing friction for trusted users while tightening scrutiny for suspicious ones.

Behavioral analytics is one of the key tools in this approach. These systems observe how users type, swipe, navigate, and transact, building models that distinguish regular activity from potential threats. If a user's behavior deviates sharply from their usual pattern, additional verification can be triggered, without burdening most legitimate customers.

Machine learning models, trained on historical fraud and user data, help identify patterns that human reviewers or basic rule engines might miss. These models evolve constantly, learning from every new attack, false decline, or chargeback. They don't just detect fraud, they forecast it.

Contextual verification adds another layer of intelligence. Instead of asking every user for a password and one-time code, systems analyze the device being used, the IP location, the session history, and even the time of day to assess risk. If someone logs in from their usual phone at a familiar location, the platform may allow a frictionless experience. But a login from a new device in a foreign country at 3 a.m.? That might trigger additional checks.

Layered defenses are essential. No single system, model, or process is perfect, and so prevention strategies are most effective when multiple safeguards are stacked. If one line of defense fails, another catches the breach before it escalates.

Fraudsters evolve constantly. They probe for weaknesses, study defenses, and adapt with speed. To stay ahead, platforms must do the same. That's why fraud prevention isn't just a compliance function or a cost center; it's a competitive advantage when executed well. A secure, seamless experience builds trust and confidence not just for regulators and partners, but for users themselves.

Fraud and cyber threats aren't theoretical. They're persistent, adaptive, and relentless. Staying ahead means investing in intelligence, automation, and readiness. Because in payments, the attacks never stop, and neither can your defenses.

Next, we shift from risk detection to risk obligation: the regulatory and legal requirements that may not try to break in but can shut your business down if ignored.

Regulatory and Compliance Risk

In payments, what you don't know can hurt you, especially when it comes to regulation. While fraudsters may exploit technical weaknesses, regulators enforce legal and operational accountability, often with little warning and high stakes. Regulatory and compliance risk isn't as flashy as cyber threats, but it can be just as devastating. A missed filing, unregistered activity, or faulty KYC process can result in fines, forced shutdowns, or permanent reputational damage.

Modern payments platforms operate across multiple geographies, regulatory frameworks, and product types, which means compliance is not one-size-fits-all. A product that's legal in one region may be banned in another. A merchant that's low risk in one sector may be flagged as high-risk elsewhere. Regulators expect companies not only to understand these distinctions but to prove compliance with audit-ready precision.

Core Areas of Exposure

AML (Anti-Money Laundering): Regulators require platforms to detect, flag, and report suspicious behavior that could indicate money laundering, terrorism financing, or organized crime. This means having automated transaction monitoring, documented escalation paths, and clear Suspicious Activity Reporting (SAR) workflows.

KYC (Know Your Customer): Failure to adequately verify user identities, especially in a digital or cross-border environment, opens the door to synthetic fraud, shell accounts, and illegal transactions. Many enforcement actions stem from onboarding practices that failed to catch bad actors early.

Sanctions Compliance (e.g., OFAC): Platforms must screen users and transactions against global sanctions lists. A single unauthorized transaction with a blocked country, person, or entity can trigger investigation and penalties, even if the breach was unintentional.

Licensing and Registration: Depending on the district, payment facilitators, money transmitters, and e-wallet providers may be required to register with financial regulators, obtain licenses, or file periodic disclosures. Operating without proper documentation, even temporarily, can result in shutdowns or delayed product launches.

When Innovation Outpaces Regulation

One of the most significant tensions in payments is that technology moves faster than the law. Many platforms launch features, such as embedded finance, instant lending, or crypto-based payments, before regulations are fully defined. While this creates opportunity, it also introduces regulatory ambiguity.

Some companies attempt to avoid oversight by operating in a gray zone. But most eventually find that proactive engagement with regulators, including sandbox programs, compliance partnerships, and transparent data sharing, builds longer-term resilience and trust.

Regulatory risk also increases as platforms scale across borders. A PSP may be compliant in its home market but face new obligations in Europe (under PSD2), Brazil (under Pix and data laws), or the U.S. (under state money transmitter rules). Keeping up with this requires more than legal counsel; it requires cross-functional coordination across compliance, engineering, and product teams.

Audits, Penalties, and Unseen Costs

In the regulatory world, enforcement is often reactive. Most interventions don't begin with a routine check-in; they start with a trigger: a data breach, a whistleblower report, a pattern of consumer complaints, or an unexpected compliance lapse. Once a regulator steps in, the burden shifts to the company to prove that its policies were not only well-documented but also actively enforced and auditable. Failing to do so can have far-reaching consequences.

The most visible outcomes are financial. Regulatory fines can easily reach into the millions, especially when violations involve data privacy, anti-money laundering (AML), or consumer protection rules. But monetary penalties are often just the start. Enforcement actions can also lead to the temporary loss of processing privileges, revoked licenses, or the imposition of remediation mandates, requiring companies to rebuild parts of their compliance programs under the supervision of third-party auditors.

Even when penalties are modest, the internal toll can be significant. Investigations divert leadership focus away from strategy and innovation. Engineering and product teams may be pulled into retrospective data pulls or urgent compliance retrofits. Investor confidence may waver. Partners may pause integrations or re-evaluate risk exposure. What starts as a procedural inquiry can ripple through an entire organization's momentum and morale.

That's why regulatory and compliance risk is not optional; it is a constant, underlying part of operating in financial services. It's not a question of if your platform will face scrutiny, but when. Every system you build, every data field you store, and every operational shortcut you consider will eventually be subject to review.

Resilient payments companies recognize this reality. They treat compliance not as a barrier to innovation, but as infrastructure, woven into product design, vendor selection, user experience, and governance. This proactive mindset turns compliance from a defensive necessity into a strategic asset that builds trust, protects licenses, and creates long-term market advantage.

Next, we shift from the risks that can be fined or fixed to one that can quietly destroy trust: reputational risk.

Reputational Risk

Some risks hit your bottom line. Reputational risk hits everything else. It affects customer trust, partner confidence, regulatory relationships, and long-term brand value. And unlike fraud or chargebacks, the damage is often amplified by how it's perceived, not just what occurred.

In the payments industry, where trust is the currency, reputational risk can stem from events large and small, such as a data breach, a delayed payout, a misleading marketing claim, or a controversial merchant onboarding. Even if financial loss is limited, the impact on public perception, media coverage, and industry trust can be severe and lasting.

Where Reputational Risk Comes From

Fraud Events: If a platform is seen as enabling or failing to prevent fraud, especially against vulnerable populations, the fallout can be swift. Media outlets, consumer watchdogs, and competitors may all use the opportunity to cast doubt on platform safety.

Regulatory Violations: Enforcement actions are public. When regulators issue fines or sanctions, the headlines often reach farther than the actual infraction. For startups or scaling platforms, this can delay partnerships, scare investors, and chill merchant acquisition.

Merchant Behavior: Onboarding a merchant that sells counterfeit goods, promotes hate speech, or engages in deceptive practices can backfire, even if the platform was unaware. Card networks may issue warnings, while consumers demand accountability.

Platform Failures: Outages, missed payments, or sudden changes to terms of service can erode user trust, especially if communication is poor or defensive. In payments, reliability is reputational equity. Every incident puts it at risk.

Public Narrative: Sometimes, it's not the event but the reaction that defines the damage. A breach that's managed transparently and promptly may build trust. One that's denied or downplayed may spark a firestorm. In a hyper-connected world, your brand's response often matters more than the root cause.

Measuring the Intangible

Reputational risk is one of the most challenging forms of exposure to measure, yet it can have some of the most immediate and lasting consequences. There's no balance sheet entry for public perception, and no dashboard that can fully capture lost trust. But when reputational damage occurs, the impact reverberates across every corner of a business.

Customer churn often rises first. Users lose confidence in the platform's security, reliability, or values, and quietly move elsewhere. The cost of acquiring new merchants increases as trust must be rebuilt, sometimes one relationship at a time. Banks and strategic partners may respond with tighter underwriting, heightened oversight, or delayed approvals, forcing the platform to absorb additional compliance burden.

Reputation also affects internal momentum. Companies under scrutiny often struggle to recruit top talent, especially for risk-sensitive roles like legal, security, and product leadership. Market expansion plans may be paused, postponed, or blocked entirely by wary regulators or cautious investors. Even if no fines are issued and no license is revoked, reputational damage can slow growth and erode long-term value.

Because of its intangible nature, reputational risk demands proactive monitoring. Innovative platforms track signals, including spikes in support tickets, rising chargeback rates, shifts in social media sentiment, and patterns in app store reviews. Media coverage, whether justified or misinformed, can rapidly reshape perception, especially in an industry where trust is foundational.

Ultimately, reputation is not managed through marketing; it's earned through consistency, transparency, and accountability. The platforms that thrive over time are those that treat reputational risk not as a PR concern, but as a core business risk, monitored, managed, and designed against, just like fraud, compliance, or operational failure.

Mitigation and Response

Reputational resilience isn't something that can be manufactured in the moment; it's the product of long-term consistency, evaluated in times of crisis. When things go wrong, as they inevitably do in any fast-moving platform environment, the difference between a contained issue and a public firestorm often comes down to preparation, communication, and values in action.

Proactive transparency is the first and most powerful defense. Companies that are clear about their policies, especially around fraud, compliance, dispute resolution, and customer support, earn credibility before a crisis ever begins. Transparency doesn't mean oversharing, but it does mean being honest and timely when expectations are not met.

Crisis planning is essential. The time to figure out who speaks on behalf of the company, what they say, and how affected parties are informed and supported is not after headlines start to circulate. Mature organizations develop clear response protocols that include external communications, internal briefings, and customer remediation workflows. When everyone knows their role, execution is faster, calmer, and more credible.

Stakeholder alignment is critical during high-stakes incidents. Legal, communications, compliance, operations, and executive leadership must work in lockstep, speaking with one voice, sharing accurate data, and responding decisively. Fragmented responses create confusion, delay trust restoration, and often compound the reputational hit.

At the foundation of it all is ethical culture. The strongest reputations are built before they're needed, through responsible onboarding, fair product design, strong governance, and visible accountability. When problems arise, a company with a consistent track record of acting with integrity will be judged more favorably, not because they're flawless, but because they've built goodwill through consistent, values-driven decisions.

Reputational risk isn't just about public image. It's about trust at scale, and in the payments world, trust isn't a feature. It's the product. Everything else rides on that foundation.

Chapter Summary: Understanding the Shape of Risk

Payments may appear simple on the surface: a swipe, a tap, a confirmation, but beneath that surface is a complex, interconnected risk environment. Each transaction moves through a gauntlet of potential exposures: financial losses, operational failures, cyber threats, regulatory missteps, and reputational consequences. No platform is immune, and no risk lives in isolation.

Financial risks show up in real-time, in losses, disputes, and liquidity constraints. Operational risks are often quieter but no less dangerous, lurking in processes, systems, and vendor dependencies. Fraud and cyber risks are dynamic, adversarial, and constantly evolving. Regulatory and compliance risks carry legal weight, and reputational risk rides on public perception, both often triggered not by the event itself, but by how it's managed.

Together, these risks form a constantly shifting landscape. What makes modern payment platforms resilient isn't just the ability to respond; it's the ability to anticipate, detect, and adapt before failure happens.

Risk management in payments is no longer a back-office function. It's a core business capability, woven into product design, engineering decisions, customer experiences, and company culture. It's not about eliminating risk, but about understanding its nature, its signals, and how it connects to everything else.

In the chapters ahead, we'll shift from theory to application, exploring how payment platforms build effective risk frameworks, implement real-time monitoring, and operationalize controls that scale with their ambition.

Because managing risk isn't just a regulatory obligation, it's how modern payments businesses survive, compete, and lead.

Section 2: Core Risk Management Frameworks

Chapter 3: Building an Effective Framework

If Chapter 2 helped us understand what risk looks like in the payments industry, Chapter 3 is about answering a more urgent question: what do we do about it?

Practical Examples in Payments

Risk in payments is dynamic, not a fixed target but a moving, evolving set of threats shaped by behavior, regulation, velocity, and scale. It cannot be managed reactively or in silos. To be effective, risk management must be systematic, embedded, and continuously adaptive. That's where a robust framework comes in.

A risk management framework is more than a set of policies or tools; it's the architecture that defines how risk is identified, categorized, measured, monitored, escalated, and mitigated across an organization. It brings structure to uncertainty and transforms reactive firefighting into proactive resilience.

In this chapter, we'll explore how payments companies, from fintech startups to global PSPs, can design frameworks that are fit for purpose, scale with complexity, and align with both commercial goals and regulatory obligations.

We'll cover key components such as:

➢ Defining risk appetite and risk ownership

➢ Structuring a three-line-of-defense model

➢ Integrating real-time risk signals into decision-making

➢ Designing effective governance and escalation paths

➢ Embedding risk thinking into product and engineering

This isn't about creating a theoretical model for a board deck. It's about building a practical operating system for managing uncertainty in one of the fastest-moving, highest-stakes industries on the planet.

Let's begin with the foundation: how to define and align your organization's risk appetite, and why it must be more than a paragraph in a compliance manual.

Defining Risk Appetite and Ownership

Every payments business assumes risk; that's a given. The real questions are: how much risk is acceptable, what kinds of risk align with your strategy, and who makes those decisions? These questions are at the heart of a company's risk appetite, the set of boundaries that define how far the business is willing to go in pursuit of growth, innovation, and efficiency, while remaining within safe and responsible limits.

Too often, risk appetite is treated as a theoretical exercise, a one-page statement buried deep within a compliance manual, rarely referenced and even less frequently updated. But in practice, a well-defined risk appetite should serve as a living guidepost. It should shape who you choose to onboard as merchants, how much credit exposure you're willing to extend, how aggressively you pursue fraud prevention, and how much friction you're eager to introduce into your user experience in the name of safety.

A strong risk appetite framework brings clarity to complex trade-offs. It helps answer critical questions, such as whether we are willing to serve high-risk merchant verticals like travel or crypto. If so, under what controls, limits, or reserves? How much financial loss, measured as a percentage of revenue or in absolute terms, is tolerable before we escalate or intervene? What level of false positives in our fraud systems is acceptable if it means reducing customer churn? And how quickly should potential regulatory inquiries or negative media coverage be escalated to executive leadership?

The answers to these questions will vary depending on the company's business model, regulatory environment, and stage of growth. A venture-backed startup, for instance, may be comfortable absorbing higher fraud losses in exchange for rapid user acquisition. Meanwhile, a publicly regulated institution might prioritize conservative controls, even at the cost of speed or conversion.

What matters most is alignment. Risk appetite must be understood and embraced across leadership, product, compliance, and operations. It cannot live in a vacuum. It must evolve alongside the business, revisited regularly as the platform scales, enters new markets, or encounters new forms of risk. Defining your appetite isn't just about avoiding danger; it's about knowing when to lean in, when to pull back, and how to do both with intention and confidence.

Ownership: Who Makes the Call?

Defining a company's risk appetite is essential, but it's only half the equation. Just as important is determining who owns risk across the organization. In modern payments, risk doesn't reside solely in the compliance department. It's embedded in every decision, system, and customer interaction. As platforms scale, effective risk management must be distributed, not centralized, with ownership clearly defined across teams.

In the most effective organizations, risk is shared across three core dimensions:

Product and Engineering own how risk is introduced and managed through user flows, onboarding experiences, API design, and platform logic. The way a product is built, from authentication mechanisms to refund handling, defines how exposed or resilient it is by default.

Operations and Customer Support determine how risk manifests in practice, encompassing exception handling, manual reviews, escalations, and day-to-day policies. These teams are often the first to notice edge cases, abuse patterns, or friction points that hint at deeper systemic issues.

Legal, Risk, and Compliance own the frameworks and governance that keep everything aligned. They define policy boundaries, monitor behavior against those guardrails, and ensure the platform stays within regulatory expectations. Their job is not to say "no", but to help the business understand the cost, consequence, and contingency of saying "yes."

Some companies formalize these responsibilities using the three lines of defense model:

The first line, typically the business and product team, owns and manages risk directly as part of execution.

The second line, consisting of risk, legal, and compliance, provides oversight, defines standards, and challenges decision-making when necessary.

The third line, often internal audit or independent assessors, offers objective assurance, testing whether controls work and policies are truly followed.

This model is most effective when roles are clearly defined, communication flows both bottom-up and top-down, and no team operates in isolation. Transparency, alignment, and shared accountability are what allow organizations to take bold steps without blind spots.

Ultimately, risk appetite is not about being risk-averse; it's about being intentional. It empowers companies to grow quickly and confidently, knowing exactly what risks they're taking, where those risks are concentrated, and what signals should trigger a response.

With ownership distributed and boundaries defined, the next step is operationalizing that framework, building a scalable system that can detect, measure, and respond to risk in real time.

The Three Lines of Defense

Once risk appetite is defined and ownership is aligned, the question becomes: How do we organize ourselves to manage risk at scale? This is where the three lines of defense model offers a practical framework, not as a rigid hierarchy, but to clarify responsibilities, reduce blind spots, and build accountability across the business.

Initially developed in the banking sector, the three lines of defense model has since become a go-to structure for risk management in payments, fintech, and embedded finance. Its power lies in separating risk into distinct functions, each with a clear role, vantage point, and level of control.

First Line: The Front Line, Business Ownership of Risk

The first line of defense in any risk management model consists of the people who are closest to day-to-day execution: the product managers designing features, the engineers building infrastructure, the operations teams onboarding merchants, and the customer support representatives managing user issues in real time. These are the teams that bring the business to life, and, in doing so, create or inherit the most immediate forms of risk.

Because they operate where strategy meets execution, the first line bears responsibility for embedding safety and control directly into the business. This includes designing user flows that are secure, compliant, and resilient, minimizing opportunities for fraud, abuse, or regulatory failure. It also means executing key risk-related policies, such as setting transaction limits, applying onboarding controls, and enforcing authentication rules, not as abstract requirements, but as real-world behaviors and tools.

Frontline teams are often the first to notice when something's off. Whether it's an uptick in support tickets, a pattern of chargebacks, or unexpected system behavior, they play a key role in surfacing edge cases and emerging issues. When trained and connected to the broader risk framework, they become an early warning system, spotting signals that more centralized teams might miss.

Most critically, the first line is tasked with making real-time decisions that align with the company's risk appetite. They're the ones who decide whether to approve an exception, flag a suspicious account, or launch a new feature with the proper safeguards in place. These choices may seem tactical in the moment, but they shape risk exposure every day.

If the first line fails, if issues go unflagged, guardrails are bypassed, or decisions are made without context, risk doesn't just remain theoretical. It materializes. That's why frontline teams must be equipped and empowered, not just trained to recognize risk, but resourced to act on it. When risk awareness is built into daily operations, platforms can move fast without losing sight of control.

The Front Line

While the first line owns and manages risk in the flow of daily operations, the second line of defense provides the structure, guidance, and oversight to ensure those frontline decisions are aligned with company strategy and regulatory expectations. This line is typically composed of legal, compliance, risk, and governance teams, the groups responsible for translating abstract requirements into concrete policies, frameworks, and accountability mechanisms.

The second line plays a critical advisory and oversight role. It defines the company's risk appetite and sets the rules that govern behavior: what types of merchants can be onboarded, what documentation is required for compliance, how transaction monitoring is implemented, and how suspicious activity is escalated. These teams don't operate the controls directly, but they ensure the proper controls exist and that business teams use them correctly.

They also maintain a cross-functional view of risk, watching for systemic vulnerabilities that individual teams might miss. A spike in support tickets, a rise in fraud losses, or a slowdown in regulatory filings may not raise alarms in isolation, but the second line is positioned to connect the dots and raise flags early.

Second Line: Governance and Accountability

Beyond policy, the second line ensures governance and accountability. It facilitates risk reviews, monitors KPIs and KRIs (key risk indicators), and ensures that issues identified by frontline teams are addressed in a timely and consistent manner. These teams are also responsible for internal reporting, helping leadership, regulators, and board members understand where risk is accumulating and how it's being managed.

Significantly, the second line operates as both a partner and a challenger. It must be close enough to the business to offer practical guidance, yet independent enough to say no when necessary. The healthiest organizations don't treat compliance or risk oversight as a bottleneck, but as a strategic function, one that protects the platform's license to operate and enables sustainable growth.

When the second line is strong, frontline teams have transparent, fair, and enforceable guardrails. When it's weak, controls become inconsistent, and risks multiply in the gaps. Oversight isn't about slowing down the business; it's about ensuring it can move forward without stepping off a cliff.

Third Line: Independent Assurance, Audit, and Accountability

The third line of defense exists to answer a critical question: *Are we doing what we said we would do, and is it working?* This line provides independent assurance through internal audit functions, external reviews, and regulatory examinations. Its role isn't to create or operate controls, but to assess whether the systems designed by the first and second lines are functioning as intended, and to surface gaps that may not be visible to those working inside the process.

Internal audit teams typically report directly to the board or audit committee, giving them the independence needed to evaluate risk objectively. They conduct deep dives into specific areas, such as merchant onboarding, AML compliance, data retention practices, or fraud case resolution, using both qualitative assessments and quantitative testing to evaluate effectiveness. Their findings don't just confirm compliance; they often reveal process inefficiencies, overlooked vulnerabilities, or risk accumulations that haven't yet materialized into problems.

External audits, penetration tests, and regulator-driven assessments serve a similar function, bringing in outside perspectives and benchmarking the company's controls against broader industry standards. These reviews often provide a level of credibility and validation that internal teams alone cannot, especially when dealing with investors, partners, or government bodies.

The third line also plays a key role in closing the loop on risk management. It ensures that issues raised during audits are tracked to resolution, that root causes are addressed (not just symptoms), and that improvements are embedded into operational and governance practices.

A strong audit function turns one-time lessons into lasting safeguards.

Crucially, the third line is most effective when it's integrated, not isolated. While it must remain independent in structure, it should be closely informed by the business's evolving risk profile, strategic goals, and operational realities. When audit is viewed as a partner in improvement, rather than just a post-mortem enforcer, it becomes a force multiplier for resilience.

The three lines of defense work best when all are clearly defined, well-staffed, and actively communicating. Risk doesn't respect organizational silos, and neither should your defense model.

Bringing It Together: From Framework to Function

The three lines of defense model is only as effective as the clarity with which it's implemented and the consistency with which it's lived. Risk cannot be managed by one team alone; it must be embedded across the organization, from the engineers who build products to the legal teams who interpret regulations and the auditors who validate the system's integrity.

When the first line is empowered to act, the second line is aligned to guide, and the third line is resourced to validate, risk becomes not just manageable, but measurable, traceable, and actionable. It creates a shared language across departments, builds institutional memory, and fosters a culture where risks are surfaced early, and decisions are made with confidence.

But a framework, even a strong one, is not enough on its own. The next challenge is operationalizing it, building the systems, dashboards, workflows, and feedback loops that allow risk to be detected, measured, and managed in real time.

That's where we turn next: from theory to execution, and from policy to platform.

Building a Scalable Risk Operating Model

A risk framework sets the vision. But it's the operating model that makes it real. In fast-growing payments platforms, where money moves instantly, regulations evolve constantly, and threats shift by the hour, managing risk cannot rely on static documents, siloed teams, or manual reviews. It requires an adaptive system: one that can detect risk in real time, measure its potential impact, route it to the right people, and trigger the correct response, all at scale.

A scalable risk operating model brings together people, process, and technology into a unified engine. It defines who watches for what, how signals are prioritized, how decisions are made, and how interventions are recorded and improved over time. Done well, it transforms risk from a reactive function into a strategic advantage, enabling speed, compliance, and trust without compromise.

Core components of this model typically include:

Signal ingestion and normalization involve pulling in data from various sources, including user behavior, transaction patterns, support tickets, onboarding flows, and infrastructure logs, and then standardizing it into a format that risk tools and teams can interpret.

Real-time decision engines, rule-based or machine learning–driven systems that evaluate activity as it happens, flag anomalies, and enforce automated responses such as holds, escalations, or notifications.

Escalation playbooks are clearly defined workflows that dictate who act when certain risk thresholds are crossed, how incidents are triaged, and what communication protocols are triggered.

Dashboards and reporting, live visibility into key risk metrics, trends, backlogs, and unresolved exceptions, tailored for operations teams, compliance officers, and executive leadership.

Feedback loops, continuous learning cycles where outputs from fraud investigations, regulatory reviews, or operational incidents are fed back into policies, scoring models, and system rules.

Importantly, scalability doesn't just mean volume. It means flexibility, the ability to adapt as new risks emerge, new geographies are entered, or new business lines are launched. The strongest risk operating models are modular, API-driven, and deeply integrated into the platform's core infrastructure, not bolted on as an afterthought.

Risk isn't static, and your systems can't be either. The goal of the operating model is to make risk visible, actionable, and accountable at every layer of the business, from frontline decisions to board-level oversight.

Signal Sources and Risk Detection

Every risk decision starts with a signal. In a payments platform, those signals don't just come from fraud alerts or compliance audits; they emerge from hundreds of places, often buried in the normal rhythm of the business. The key to building a responsive risk operating model is knowing where to listen, how to interpret what you hear, and how to distinguish meaningful risk signals from everyday noise.

Effective platforms aggregate signals from across five primary domains:

User behavior and platform activity encompass various metrics, including login patterns, session frequency, device changes, payment velocity, and interaction flows. Sudden shifts in behavior, like a user who usually transacts locally now sending large international payments, may indicate fraud, account takeover, or policy circumvention.

Transaction and financial data, Payment patterns, refund rates, chargeback trends, and funding anomalies often point to emerging credit or fraud exposure. Spikes in failed payments, abnormal success rates, or inconsistent disbursement behavior can highlight broken flows or coordinated abuse.

Operational workflows, Manual reviews, support tickets, exception queues, and escalations are critical early-warning systems. If the same issue surfaces repeatedly across merchants or users, it may reveal a systemic vulnerability that hasn't yet triggered a formal alert.

Third-party integrations and vendor data, along with Signals from KYC providers, banking partners, or fraud prevention vendors, help validate onboarding quality, transaction legitimacy, or AML screening coverage. Discrepancies between systems, such as mismatched user data or conflicting fraud scores, often serve as early indicators of risk buildup.

External sources, public blocklists, social media chatter, app store reviews, news mentions, and regulatory bulletins provide essential context. A merchant suddenly mentioned in a legal filing, or a new fraud trend circulating online, may call for immediate action, even before internal metrics respond.

The challenge isn't just collecting these signals; it's normalizing, prioritizing, and connecting them. Risk data often lives in different systems, owned by other teams. Building connectors, pipelines, and normalization logic is a foundational investment. It allows platforms to develop a unified risk intelligence layer, where alerts are evaluated not in isolation, but in context, helping teams spot the difference between an edge case and the start of a pattern.

Ultimately, strong detection starts with strong signal hygiene. If you can't see it, you can't measure it, and if you can't measure it, you can't manage it.

Cross-Functional Visibility

Real-time monitoring works best when shared across functions. Product teams learn where risk enters the user flow. Ops teams understand where bottlenecks live. Compliance sees where thresholds are being pushed. Executives spot macro trends that affect the business model itself.

This creates a culture of active risk ownership, where no one waits for the audit report to see what went wrong. Instead, everyone sees risk unfolding and knows what to do about it.

Building real-time monitoring is like building radar. You don't just want to know where you are, you want to know what's coming. And in payments, the storms form fast.

With real-time visibility in place, the next step is building a governance system that ensures those insights lead to measured, accountable action. That's where we turn next: escalation paths, risk committees, and governance models that keep the system aligned.

Governance, Escalation, and Cross-Functional Alignment

Even the best risk signals are useless if no one acts on them. Governance bridges the gap between insight and intervention, ensuring that when risk emerges, it's not just detected, but addressed quickly, consistently, and with the right level of authority. In a payments organization, where decisions often involve product, legal, operations, and compliance teams, governance is not a bureaucratic layer; it's the connective tissue that enables alignment, accountability, and speed.

Without a strong governance model, risk becomes fragmented. Alerts accumulate without resolution. Policies are applied inconsistently across teams or regions. Ownership becomes unclear. Escalations stall in limbo, not due to apathy, but because no one has the mandate or clarity to make the call. When a real crisis hits, a regulatory notice, a merchant fraud event, or a data breach, the result is often confusion and delay, not because of negligence, but because governance wasn't built for scale.

That's why a well-defined escalation framework is at the heart of operational governance. When a risk threshold is crossed, whether a merchant exceeds chargeback limits, a fraud ring is identified, or a sensitive regulatory notice is received, there must be no ambiguity about what happens next.

Effective escalation frameworks answer five core questions:

1.   Ownership must be pre-defined, not debated in the moment.

2.   Teams should know their boundaries: what they can resolve and when to elevate.

3.   Thresholds should be clear, whether based on volume, velocity, dollar value, or reputational impact, along with specific routes for internal communication.

4.   Every material risk event should generate a consistent paper trail: what was discovered, what action was taken, and what gaps were identified.

5.   Risk doesn't wait for meetings. Temporary limits, holds, or locks may be necessary to contain exposure while a deeper review occurs.

Escalation doesn't need to be slow or overly formal. The best frameworks are structured but flexible. Not every incident requires a war room or executive briefing, but every team should know what qualifies as a material risk and when it's time to raise the flag. That cultural clarity turns governance from a bottleneck into an enabler: one that keeps decisions moving, surfaces issues early, and ensures the entire business stays coordinated.

Risk Committees: Aligning Risk Appetite and Trade-Offs

To bring structure to complex risk decisions, many organizations establish a risk committee. This cross-functional group meets regularly to review elevated issues, assess policy proposals, and align business strategy with the organization's defined risk appetite. Far from being a procedural formality, a well-run risk committee acts as a central nervous system for risk governance, helping the business navigate trade-offs with clarity, speed, and accountability.

These committees typically include representatives from product, compliance, legal, finance, engineering, and executive leadership. The frequency of meetings may vary, weekly, monthly, or on an ad hoc basis. Still, the agenda remains consistent: to evaluate meaningful risk exposures and decide whether current controls are sufficient, or whether action is needed.

A mature risk committee tackles questions that no single department can resolve in isolation. For instance:

Can a new product launch under existing risk controls? If not, what needs to be added, and how soon?

Does a proposed merchant vertical, such as gaming, adult content, or crypto, exceed the company's risk appetite? If the exposure is significant, are there safeguards that can bring it within acceptable limits?

Are fraud rules unintentionally suppressing growth? If conversion is dropping due to false positives or friction-heavy flows, should the system be recalibrated, and what loss thresholds are acceptable?

In these discussions, the risk committee acts as both a referee and a translator, balancing the ambitions of growth teams with the guardrails of compliance, and ensuring that trade-offs are surfaced and discussed explicitly, not passively absorbed. When run well, the committee fosters alignment and agility, empowering teams to move forward with confidence, knowing their decisions are grounded in shared understanding.

Critically, a risk committee doesn't exist to prevent risk; it exists to manage it intentionally. It ensures the organization is making conscious choices about how much risk it's willing to accept, what protections are in place, and what early warning signs will trigger a change in posture.

Responding to Change: New Regulations, Market Shifts, and Partner Risk

One of the most valuable functions of a risk committee, and governance more broadly, is its ability to serve as a strategic escalation point for fast-moving or cross-cutting challenges. Whether it's a newly issued regulation, a shift in partner risk posture, or a sudden market disruption, the governance group provides a structured forum for evaluating impact, urgency, and response across functions.

This group typically includes leadership from risk, compliance, product, operations, legal, and finance. Together, they function as guardians of the risk appetite, ensuring decisions are made with complete context, not in isolated silos. They help translate regulatory shifts into operational requirements, partner feedback into contractual guardrails, and market signals into proactive policy reviews.

But governance doesn't just live inside meeting rooms. It plays out in the daily rhythm of execution, in how product roadmaps are prioritized, how engineering teams deploy code, how customer support resolves edge cases, and how finance models reserves and exposure.

That's why effective risk teams don't operate at the edges of the business. They embed across it, translating risk into practical business terms and partnering with teams to navigate trade-offs in real time. They aren't just reporters of risk; they are facilitators of decisions.

For example:

Working with the product to strike the right balance between frictionless onboarding and robust identity verification.

Collaborating with operations to refine manual review queues, triage exceptions, and manage queues more intelligently.

Supporting engineering with tooling to detect fraud signals, prevent API abuse, and monitor integrity at the system level.

Partnering with finance to model chargeback exposure, reserve scenarios, and capital adequacy under stress.

This kind of cross-functional alignment doesn't slow down decision-making; it gives it structure. It ensures that when risk is taken, it's taken with intention, with clear ownership, and with contingencies in place.

In fast-moving payments organizations, governance isn't about eliminating mistakes. Mistakes will happen.

Governance is about catching them early, correcting them quickly, and learning from them, so they don't become systemic.

Next, we explore how to take governance and monitoring even further by embedding risk thinking directly into product and engineering decisions, long before the first transaction is ever processed.

Embedding Risk into Product and Engineering

Risk management doesn't start at the point of transaction; it begins much earlier, in how platforms are built. Every payment flow, every onboarding screen, every API endpoint is a potential entry point for exposure. That's why the most resilient payment companies embed risk not just in monitoring and compliance, but in product and engineering design.

For too long, risk was treated as a final checkpoint, a review before launch, a gatekeeper to innovation. But in today's environment, that model breaks down. Product cycles are faster, engineering teams are decentralized, and features evolve weekly. The old model of "build now, review later" leads to blind spots, rework, and emergency patches.

Modern risk frameworks shift left, bringing risk thinking upstream, into the very architecture of product development.

Risk-Aware Product Design

Product managers hold the keys to how users interact with a platform, and in payments, those interactions are often the very points where risk begins. Fraud, abuse, regulatory violations, and financial loss rarely originate from a system failure alone. More often, they stem from design decisions made without fully considering how the feature might be exploited, misused, or misunderstood at scale.

Take, for example, a referral program that unintentionally incentivizes synthetic identities. Or an onboarding flow that skips document verification in high-risk geographies because speed was prioritized over scrutiny. Alternatively, a payment button that allows high-value transactions to proceed without confirmation could open the door to errors or misuse. Even a generous refund policy, if not properly gated, can quietly fuel large-scale friendly fraud that's difficult to detect until the damage is done.

None of these are engineering flaws; they're product design choices. And while each may have been built with the user in mind, they reveal how easily risk can be introduced when features are developed in a vacuum. That's why the most resilient product teams are those who apply a risk lens from day one.

Risk-aware product design doesn't mean turning every planning meeting into a compliance review. It means building with foresight. It means stepping back during ideation and asking: how might a bad actor exploit this? What happens if a user misuses this feature at scale? Do we have the visibility to monitor for abuse once this goes live? And is this flow aligned with the company's broader risk appetite and regulatory obligations?

In practice, these questions often uncover necessary refinements, a frictionless flow that needs a soft control, a promotion that needs eligibility thresholds, or a back end that needs better logging. These aren't barriers to innovation. They're safeguards that allow innovation to scale without compromise.

Risk-aware design is not about being cautious; it's about being smart. It shifts the goal from simply shipping features to shipping features that can withstand pressure, resist abuse, and hold up to scrutiny. And in doing so, it transforms risk from a reactive clean-up effort into a proactive design constraint, one that ultimately makes the platform stronger, not slower.

Engineering with Risk in Mind

If product teams define the experience, engineering teams build the foundation. They control the infrastructure, logic, and integrations that make a platform work, or, if neglected, leave it exposed. From payment processing and authentication to vendor connections and system monitoring, engineering owns the code paths where risk either enters or is stopped cold.

Embedding risk into engineering isn't just about shipping secure code; it's about designing systems that can detect, respond to, and recover from failure. That starts with visibility. Without comprehensive, accessible, and secure logging, incidents are more complex to trace, abuse patterns go undetected, and accountability is compromised. Audit trails are not optional; they're the backbone of trust and response readiness.

Resilience also depends on how systems are structured. APIs must be designed not just for speed and functionality, but for safety. Input validation, authentication layers, and abuse prevention mechanisms must be native, not bolted on later. When APIs are left unguarded, they become targets for injection attacks, enumeration, or transaction replay.

Control of platform logic is another line of defense. Sensitive actions, like password resets, login attempts, or payment retries, must be rate-limited to prevent brute-force attacks or bot-driven fraud. These protections aren't simply good security hygiene; they're essential controls for risk mitigation at scale.

Equally important are the internal response mechanisms. Engineering teams should build in kill switches, escalation hooks, and circuit breakers, tools that allow rapid containment when abuse or system anomalies are detected. In a real-time environment, the ability to throttle or halt risky behavior in minutes can mean the difference between a contained incident and a platform-wide breach.

Risk-conscious engineering also means integrating testing and policy enforcement directly into the development process. Static analysis, dependency scanning, and security validations should be part of the CI/CD pipeline, not afterthoughts added post-deployment. These tools not only catch vulnerabilities early but also reinforce a culture of accountability and quality across engineering teams.

Perhaps most importantly, engineering performance must be measured by more than feature delivery or uptime. Teams should also be judged on resilience, observability, and the strength of internal controls. A system that performs beautifully but fails silently under stress is not built for payments at scale.

When engineers build with risk in mind, platforms become safer by design, not because someone caught the problem after launch, but because the problem never made it to production in the first place.

Shared Language, Shared Success

Embedding risk into product and engineering is not just a technical challenge; it's a communication challenge. It requires a shared language between teams that often speak in different terms, prioritize different metrics, and operate on different cadences. Risk and compliance teams must learn to navigate product flows, understand architectural trade-offs, and communicate risk in the language of features, APIs, and deployment cycles. In turn, product managers and engineers must build fluency in fraud vectors, regulatory triggers, and systemic vulnerabilities, not to become experts in those fields, but to recognize when their work could introduce unintended consequences.

This kind of cross-functional fluency is a hallmark of high-performing organizations. It eliminates the friction and confusion that can otherwise derail launches, delay product rollouts, or create dangerous blind spots in live systems. It prevents the handoffs and "lost in translation" moments that lead to last-minute compliance fire drills or misaligned expectations between teams. When everyone shares the same mental model of risk and the same responsibility for managing it, risk transforms from a blocker into a design principle.

The most resilient platforms don't treat risk as someone else's job. They anticipate it on the whiteboard. They build it into test plans. They review it as part of QA. And they treat product managers and engineers not just as builders of features, but as defenders of trust, equal partners in the platform's safety, reliability, and compliance posture.

Chapter Summary: From Framework to Culture

Risk management in payments isn't just a defensive function; it's an operational strategy. In a space defined by speed, complexity, and constant threat, a strong risk framework does more than protect the business. It shapes it.

This chapter laid the groundwork for that structure. It began with the need to define risk appetite, not as legal boilerplate, but as a compass for product, compliance, and commercial trade-offs. From there, we explored how to assign clear ownership using the three lines of defense model, ensuring that risk is not relegated to the back office, but distributed across teams who make real-time decisions every day.

We emphasized the need for real-time monitoring, not just for fraud, but for behavioral shifts, partner instability, and policy violations. We examined the importance of governance, escalation protocols, and risk committees in aligning cross-functional teams around informed, timely decisions. And finally, we stressed the imperative to embed risk thinking into the heart of product and engineering, where vulnerabilities are often introduced, but where prevention can be most effective.

Together, these components form a living, breathing operating system for risk. But even the best frameworks fail without execution. In the next chapter, we move from architecture to implementation, exploring how to operationalize risk controls across people, processes, and platforms, especially as the business grows and evolves.

Because managing risk at scale isn't about perfection, it's about resilience, visibility, and alignment, at every layer of the stack.

As we move from frameworks to the front lines, Chapter 4 explores how risk strategies are embedded in real-time operations.

DAVID WEBB

Chapter 4: Operationalizing Risk Management

A framework is only as good as its execution. Policies, monitoring tools, and governance models are critical, but unless they're embedded into the daily rhythm of a payments organization, they remain theoretical. Chapter 4 is about turning risk strategy into operational reality.

In this chapter, we focus on how payment companies operationalize risk management across every level of the business, from frontline onboarding to executive oversight, from fraud rules in production to training programs in HR. We shift from understanding "what risk is" and "how risk is structured" to how risk is managed.

Risk management isn't a single team's job. It's a shared, ongoing discipline that depends on:

➢ Clear workflows and automation

➢ Cross-functional coordination

➢ Feedback loops and escalation triggers

➢ Embedded controls in tools, systems, and decision logic

➢ Team training and risk fluency at every level

We'll explore how high-performing organizations put risk controls in motion, in onboarding, transaction monitoring, fraud prevention, dispute handling, regulatory reporting, and beyond.

The focus now is on execution: building resilient systems, empowering teams, and maintaining a culture of accountability as the business scales.

Let's begin with the first primary domain: merchant and customer onboarding, where risk enters the platform.

Onboarding Controls and Risk Screening

The moment a new merchant or customer joins a payment platform, a new risk is introduced. Whether it's fraud, regulatory exposure, chargeback liability, or reputational damage, most downstream issues can be traced back to onboarding. That's why effective risk management begins not with detection, but with prevention at the front door.

Onboarding is not just about conversion speed. It's about making deliberate decisions about who you let onto your platform, how much trust you extend, and under what conditions. Every new account is a bet, and onboarding controls help you stack the odds in your favor.

Know Your Customer (KYC) and Know Your Business (KYB)

KYC and KYB are more than just regulatory checkboxes; they are foundational pillars of both compliance strategy and operational risk management. When implemented thoughtfully, they don't just satisfy legal obligations; they function as early-warning systems. These processes help platforms filter out bad actors, flag inconsistencies in identity or intent, and generate meaningful signals that often predict future behavior, long before any transaction takes place.

For individual users, KYC processes typically begin with document verification, such as passports, driver's licenses, or national IDs, used to confirm identity and match against known databases. But modern platforms often go further, incorporating biometric or liveness checks to verify that the person behind the device matches the identity being presented. Signals like IP geolocation, address consistency, device fingerprinting, and behavioral indicators are layered in to spot anomalies, such as identity theft, shared devices across accounts, or login behavior that doesn't align with stated geography.

When it comes to businesses, KYB goes even deeper. Platforms must validate corporate registration details, ensure the legitimacy of the business's existence, and understand its operating model. A key component is UBO (Ultimate Beneficial Owner) screening, which provides transparency into who controls or profits from the entity, a critical factor in identifying hidden relationships or shell structures. Sanctions screening against global watchlists (such as OFAC, EU, and UN lists) ensures the business and its owners aren't engaged in prohibited activity. Additionally, platforms often perform website reviews, service model checks, and industry-based risk scoring to evaluate reputational and compliance exposure based on geography, sector, and transaction patterns.

The challenge lies in balancing rigor with usability. KYC and KYB must be robust enough to detect real threats, yet flexible enough to support diverse user types, global geographies, and rapid onboarding. Friction should be applied where it's needed, such as for higher-risk industries, countries, or volumes, but minimized for low-risk profiles to ensure conversion and customer satisfaction.

At their best, these checks serve dual purposes: they protect the platform from financial crime, regulatory breach, and reputational harm, and they establish a foundation of trust between the platform and its users from the very first interaction.

Tiered Risk Models

In a diverse and fast-moving payments ecosystem, not every customer presents the same level of risk, and treating them all as if they do leads to inefficiency, friction, and missed signals. That's why high-performing platforms rely on tiered risk models: dynamic onboarding strategies that calibrate due diligence based on the inherent risk of the customer, their industry, geography, and behavior.

Rather than applying a one-size-fits-all onboarding process, tiered models allow platforms to scale their scrutiny. A low-volume merchant operating in a well-understood, low-risk vertical may be onboarded with minimal KYB, lighter document requirements, and automated checks, perhaps with downstream monitoring and a deferred manual review once transactions begin. These cases pose limited exposure and can be safely fast-tracked to preserve onboarding velocity.

By contrast, merchants operating in higher-risk sectors, such as crypto exchanges, firearms vendors, or nutraceutical businesses, often require a vastly different approach. These profiles may demand enhanced due diligence, including deeper UBO analysis, additional documentation, real-time screening, and external verification. Some platforms may introduce reserve requirements, conditional approval flows, or even route these applicants to executive-level review. In these cases, the onboarding process becomes a strategic gate, designed to balance opportunity with accountability.

Importantly, tiering is not just a compliance technique; it is an operational alignment tool. It ensures that a platform's risk appetite is enforced in practice, not just on paper. It also preserves internal resources, enabling fraud, risk, and compliance teams to focus on cases that genuinely require their attention, rather than expending maximum effort on minimal risk.

A well-designed tiered model enables speed without sacrificing safety. It lets platforms onboard good customers faster, while making deliberate, informed decisions about high-risk applicants. When done right, it supports growth and trust in equal measure, creating an infrastructure that can scale without cracking under the weight of complexity.

Automated Screening and Dynamic Controls

Manual reviews have their place, but they don't scale, especially in a high-growth platform handling thousands of new users or merchants daily. To manage onboarding at volume while still maintaining security and regulatory integrity, modern payments companies rely on automated screening systems that combine internal risk engines, third-party data sources, and machine learning models.

These systems don't just validate identity; they analyze patterns. They look for anomalies and inconsistencies that human reviewers might miss or only catch too late. A new merchant with a freshly registered domain, a reused phone number tied to multiple accounts, or a delivery address that overlaps with dozens of flagged profiles may not trigger alarms on their own. But in context, they form a risk signature that demands attention.

Automated screeners can detect signs of synthetic identity fraud, document tampering, or coordinated application behavior. They scan for velocity anomalies, such as bursts of signups from a single IP range, rapid credential reuse, or behavior that mimics bot-driven testing. Some systems even ingest reputational signals from scraped reviews, prior platform history, or darknet exposure, helping flag users or merchants with a known history of abuse.

When elevated risk is detected, the system responds dynamically. It might apply friction in the form of additional document requests, IP verification, or activation delays. In moderate cases, it escalates the applicant for manual review. In more severe instances, the system can automatically reject the application, save valuable time and prevent exposure before it starts.

The most effective platforms don't rely solely on fixed, rule-based systems. Instead, they invest in adaptive screening models that evolve with their risk environment. These systems learn over time, incorporating feedback from real-world fraud, adjusting thresholds based on emerging patterns, and aligning with updated compliance obligations. What may have seemed benign yesterday could raise red flags tomorrow, and platforms must be able to detect that shift as it happens.

Ultimately, automated screening is not about eliminating human oversight; it's about focusing it where it's needed most. By automating the bulk of decisions, platforms empower risk and compliance teams to engage where judgment and nuance are essential, while letting the system manage the rest with speed, consistency, and scale.

Continuous Monitoring Post-Onboarding

Onboarding is not the finish line for risk; it's the starting gate. Sophisticated actors know how to pass identity checks, submit clean documentation, and mirror the behavior of legitimate users during initial reviews. Their goal isn't to raise suspicion during onboarding. The goal is to get through undetected and act later. That's why innovative platforms invest heavily in continuous monitoring after approval, tracking behavior over time to identify emerging threats before they cause damage.

Once a customer or merchant is active, new signals emerge. Transaction velocity, volume spikes, and shifts in payment patterns offer critical insight into intent. A new merchant suddenly pushing high-value transactions, or a user drastically increasing transfer amounts, may signal fraud, money laundering, or account takeover. These patterns often appear only after the initial diligence has cleared, which is why behavioral monitoring is essential.

Other indicators include dispute frequency, sudden refund behavior, or changes in user location and device access. A surge in chargebacks or customer complaints may indicate a merchant is misrepresenting goods or failing to deliver services. Similarly, logins from unexpected geographies or IPs, particularly when tied to sensitive actions, can point to compromised accounts or credential misuse.

For merchants, monitoring goes deeper still. Changes to website content, product categories, or pricing models may suggest a pivot into prohibited or high-risk activity. A merchant that starts as a legitimate retailer could shift into gray-market sales or attempt to launder funds through rapid category hopping. Without ongoing visibility, these changes often go unnoticed until flagged by a bank, regulator, or chargeback wave.

Continuous monitoring acts as a critical second line of defense, catching issues that the onboarding process wasn't designed to see. It allows platforms to respond not to who someone says they are, but to how they behave over time. And the earlier these signals are caught, the easier they are to contain, before they become losses, investigations, or reputational incidents.

Ultimately, onboarding is the first handshake between a platform and its users. But trust is earned and evaluated long after that moment. The stronger, more intelligent, and more adaptive that first checkpoint is, the fewer crises a platform will need to clean up later.

Next, we shift to managing risk in the heart of the transaction flow, where decisions must be made in milliseconds, the stakes are high, and the cost of failure is immediate.

Static Rules vs. Adaptive Models

For many platforms, static rules were the original foundation of fraud prevention. Blocking transactions from high-risk geographies, flagging large payments, or rejecting known suspicious IP addresses are time-tested tactics that still serve a valuable purpose. But static rules have limits. Fraudsters evolve quickly, adapting to hard-coded controls by mimicking normal behavior, cycling through proxies, or spreading attacks across distributed vectors. What once seemed obvious becomes easy to mask.

That's why today's most resilient platforms don't rely on static logic alone. They supplement it with adaptive, data-driven models, intelligent systems that continuously learn from every transaction, login, and interaction. These models are designed not to follow fixed paths, but to recognize patterns and assess context. They ask: *Does this behavior look normal for this user? For this geography? For this time of day?* And when it doesn't, they act, not based on a single input, but on a composite of data points stitched together in real time.

Machine learning plays a central role in these systems. Rather than flagging only what's been seen before, modern fraud models can predict likelihood, surfacing transactions that mirror known attack strategies or deviate subtly from past behavior. These models generate risk scores that inform transaction outcomes: approve, hold, escalate, or decline. These scores aren't just binary; they allow platforms to introduce nuanced responses like applying friction, requesting step-up authentication, or limiting transaction size without outright rejection.

Over time, adaptive models become more refined. As fraud patterns shift, the system shifts with them, continuously ingesting feedback from confirmed cases, false positives, and resolution outcomes. This feedback loop enables the platform to maintain a high standard of detection without degrading the user experience.

Importantly, the best systems combine both approaches: rules for clarity and speed, models for depth and adaptability. Static rules manage known threats with immediate certainty. Adaptive models manage ambiguity, adjusting to new tactics and unfamiliar signals without requiring a complete system overhaul. Together, they create a defense that is both fast and flexible, capable of reacting to known threats and anticipating the ones yet to come.

Making Monitoring Actionable

Detection alone isn't enough. In a real-time payments environment, simply identifying risky behavior without a timely and appropriate response turns intelligence into noise. What separates effective platforms from vulnerable ones isn't just how well they detect anomalies, it's what they do next.

Once high-risk behavior is flagged, the system must decide: Is this a false alarm, a minor deviation, or an immediate threat? That decision must trigger a calibrated response, tailored to the level of risk. In some cases, the transaction may be allowed to proceed with caution, perhaps with added logging or downstream monitoring. In others, a step-up authentication may be inserted, requiring the user to validate their identity through a second factor. More serious cases may warrant real-time declines, user notifications, or immediate escalation to manual review. In extreme scenarios, such as suspected coordinated fraud or policy violations, the platform may need to freeze the account altogether.

This is where the absolute precision of a risk system is evaluated. If the logic is too aggressive, good users are caught in the net, blocked, frustrated, and potentially lost. If it's too permissive, fraud slips through, undermining trust, revenue, and platform stability. The goal isn't to overcorrect. The goal is to intervene with surgical accuracy, applying just enough friction to stop abuse without interrupting legitimate behavior.

At the core of this capability are transaction monitoring systems and velocity controls, engines that track behavior across time, user cohorts, devices, and geographies. They assess patterns in motion, not just static thresholds, and adjust posture dynamically based on context and escalation history.

These systems sit at the heart of operational risk management. They're the difference between seeing risk and containing it, between detecting threats and responding before loss occurs. When tuned correctly, they keep the platform responsive, accountable, and resilient, allowing growth at scale without compromising on security or user trust.

Disputes, Chargebacks, and Customer Claims

In the payments ecosystem, not all risks come from external threats. Some are initiated by legitimate users who become dissatisfied, confused, or opportunistic. Disputes and chargebacks are an inevitable part of doing business, but if unmanaged, they become a critical point of financial, operational, and reputational risk.

Every dispute represents a breakdown in trust: a customer didn't get what they paid for, a transaction appeared unfamiliar, or a merchant failed to meet expectations. Regardless of intent, these moments require the platform to balance consumer protection, merchant support, and fraud prevention, often under tight time pressure and scrutiny from card networks or regulators.

Understanding Chargebacks: The Mechanics

Chargebacks are one of the most visible and costly forms of downstream payment risk. At their core, a chargeback is a forced payment reversal, typically initiated by a cardholder through their issuing bank when a customer disputes a transaction due to suspected fraud, confusion, or dissatisfaction. The bank then temporarily holds the funds from the platform or merchant while the dispute is investigated. Card networks like Visa and Mastercard function as intermediaries, enforcing standardized dispute processes and often assigning liability to the merchant unless compelling evidence proves the charge was valid and properly fulfilled.

Chargebacks can originate from several sources. In cases of card-present fraud, a stolen physical card might be used in a face-to-face environment. Still, in the digital space, it's more often card-not-present fraud, where stolen credentials are used online without the cardholder's knowledge. Another major category is friendly fraud, where the customer falsely claims that a legitimate transaction was unauthorized, often to secure a refund without returning a product or canceling a service.

Some disputes stem from service-related issues: a product that never arrives, a service that fails to meet expectations, or a delivery that doesn't match the original description. Others are caused by recurring billing confusion, such as unclear subscription terms, difficulty canceling, or surprise charges after a free trial period ends. In all these scenarios, if the merchant cannot provide sufficient evidence, such as proof of delivery, clear refund policies, or user acceptance, the chargeback is upheld.

The actual cost of a chargeback goes far beyond the transaction amount. Each case carries fees, labor, and reputational damage. Platforms must absorb internal review costs, external dispute processing fees, and potential penalties from card networks if chargeback ratios exceed defined thresholds. For high-risk merchants or verticals, excessive chargebacks can trigger elevated monitoring programs or even result in processing restrictions and account termination.

Understanding how chargebacks work and why they happen is essential for designing effective dispute prevention strategies and maintaining network compliance. In the next section, we'll explore how to manage chargeback risk proactively before the dispute ever reaches the network.

Proactive Chargeback Management

While chargebacks are often treated as a downstream inevitability, the most effective platforms treat them as preventable events, signals of upstream friction, misaligned expectations, or gaps in risk controls. Managing chargeback risk begins not at the point of dispute, but at the point of design: in how products are sold, services delivered, and transactions communicated.

At the core of proactive chargeback management is clarity, ensuring customers know exactly what they're buying, when they'll be billed, and how to get support if something goes wrong. Misunderstandings about pricing, subscription renewals, or refund policies often trigger disputes that could have been avoided with better messaging. Clear terms of service, visible cancellation paths, and prompt post-purchase confirmations go a long way in reducing ambiguity, and with it, dispute volume.

Equally important is transaction visibility. Providing users with self-service access to past purchases, receipts, and billing history helps reduce the likelihood of disputing unknown charges. Many chargebacks stem from forgotten subscriptions, misidentified merchant names on statements, or a lack of a digital paper trail. When users can verify a charge independently, they're less likely to escalate through their bank.

Operationally, platforms can deploy risk scoring and velocity controls to detect chargeback-prone behavior before it becomes systemic. New users making large purchases, rapid refunds, or failed login attempts across accounts may indicate future disputes or coordinated fraud. By flagging and throttling these signals early, or applying friction like step-up authentication or manual review, platforms can deflect costly reversals later.

Some platforms also benefit from chargeback alerts through network programs, which offer early warning before a dispute becomes final. These alerts give merchants a short window to issue a proactive refund or resolution, effectively neutralizing the chargeback and reducing ratios.

Beyond prevention, evidence readiness is critical. When chargebacks do occur, platforms need to respond quickly and with precision. That means having well-documented order details, proof of delivery, terms acceptance, and support logs accessible in a standardized format, ready to be submitted with minimal delay.

Proactive chargeback management is not just about protecting revenue; it's about preserving user trust, maintaining processor relationships, and ensuring operational scalability. A platform that understands the why behind the dispute is far better positioned to prevent the next one.

Dispute Resolution Workflows

Even with the best prevention measures in place, some chargebacks will still occur. When they do, a platform's ability to respond quickly and effectively can mean the difference between recovery and loss. That's where strong dispute resolution workflows come into play, providing a structured, repeatable process for managing chargebacks at scale.

The first step is triage. Once a dispute is received, either through a card network or an alert system, the platform must determine whether it's winnable, refundable, or escalatable. Not every chargeback is worth fighting. If the evidence is weak or the customer experience broke down, issuing a refund may be the right move. But if the transaction was valid and compliant, a prompt, well-supported response can lead to reversal and recovery.

Successful disputes rely on evidence readiness. The most effective teams don't scramble for documents when a case is filed; they maintain organized, accessible records for every transaction. That includes proof of delivery, service logs, refund terms, cancellation attempts, screenshots of customer communications, and explicit acceptance of terms at checkout. This documentation is what turns a dispute from an accusation into a resolved issue.

Workflows should also include ownership and escalation paths. Chargeback cases that involve potential fraud, VIP customers, or high-value merchants may require elevated review or legal input. Others can be routed through automated response templates or resolved by support teams. Clarity around who manages what ensures that disputes don't fall between the cracks, and that they're managed within the narrow response windows required by card networks.

Metrics matter, too. Dispute win rates, response times, and root cause breakdowns should be monitored closely. A spike in friendly fraud may require changes to refund policies or customer support messaging. Repeated service complaints may highlight a product quality issue or a fulfillment gap. The dispute process isn't just defensive, it's diagnostic, revealing signals about what's broken and where to improve.

Ultimately, dispute resolution is about protecting both sides of the platform, safeguarding revenue while showing users that the platform is accountable, responsive, and fair.

Loss Forecasting and Reserve Planning

No matter how effective the controls, some level of financial loss is inevitable in payments. Chargebacks, fraud, credit risk, and operational errors all create drag on revenue, but with proper forecasting and reserve planning, these losses don't have to become destabilizing events. They can be anticipated, budgeted, and absorbed without compromising the business.

Loss forecasting begins with understanding historical patterns: How frequently do chargebacks occur, and from which merchant segments? What types of fraud lead to losses, synthetic identity abuse, account takeovers, or insider manipulation? Which cohorts present higher default risk? These trends are critical not only for budgeting but also for setting internal thresholds: How much loss is acceptable before intervention is required? What proportion of revenue can be allocated to risk absorption without cutting into the margin?

Sophisticated platforms model loss scenarios across a range of variables, transaction volume, risk tier, region, or product type. By stress-evaluating these assumptions, they can estimate the impact of spikes in disputes, shifts in fraud tactics, or regulatory changes. These forecasts are not just finance exercises; they directly inform product velocity, merchant onboarding thresholds, and even pricing strategies.

To buffer against volatility, platforms establish reserves, funds set aside to absorb anticipated losses. These may take the form of internal risk buffers or external requirements imposed by banks and card networks. For merchants, reserves might be held on a rolling basis, a percentage of revenue withheld for a defined period to cover chargebacks or reversals. For platforms, reserves ensure that a sudden wave of fraud or disputes doesn't interrupt cash flow or violate processor obligations.

Reserve planning must be dynamic. As risk exposure evolves, due to growth, new markets, or shifting fraud vectors, reserve models must adjust. Under-reserving creates exposure; over-reserving locks up capital. Striking the right balance requires real-time data, cross-functional coordination, and alignment with both financial and risk teams.

When forecasting and reserves are done well, a platform doesn't just survive risk; it absorbs it predictably, protecting users, partners, and itself from systemic shocks.

Merchant Risk Reviews and Deactivation Policies

Managing merchant risk isn't just about onboarding well; it's about staying vigilant throughout the lifecycle of the relationship. A merchant that clears initial checks may later shift into higher-risk behavior: pushing prohibited products, incurring excessive chargebacks, or pivoting to a business model that falls outside the platform's risk appetite. That's why high-performing platforms invest in ongoing merchant risk reviews and enforce structured deactivation policies when boundaries are crossed.

Merchant reviews can be triggered by time, volume, or behavior. Some platforms conduct scheduled reviews for high-risk verticals every quarter, for instance. In contrast, others initiate ad hoc reviews based on risk signals: a spike in disputes, a sudden change in transaction volume, or unusual traffic to a merchant's website. These reviews assess the merchant's ongoing compliance with platform policies, card network rules, and regulatory obligations.

Risk teams evaluate factors like chargeback ratios, refund velocity, content or product changes, and KYC data quality. A merchant who originally sold apparel but now lists high-risk supplements or adult content may raise flags. So might one who begins transacting at volumes far beyond their historical average, especially if the pattern suggests potential fraud, money laundering, or reputational exposure.

When issues are detected, the first step is often remediation. This might include merchant outreach, requests for updated documentation, onboarding a reserve, or temporary limits on transaction volume. The goal is not to punish, but to contain exposure while offering a path back to good standing, especially for merchants with otherwise strong records.

However, when the risk becomes too high or remediation fails, platforms must be willing to deactivate or offboard the merchant. This decision should be guided by clearly documented thresholds and policy frameworks, not ad hoc judgment. Deactivation criteria might include exceeding a network chargeback ratio for consecutive months, selling prohibited goods, failing to respond to compliance requests, or evidence of intentional fraud.

A strong deactivation policy is both firm and fair. It protects the platform from cascading liability, while also ensuring merchants are treated consistently and informed transparently. The best systems provide early warning, document every step, and allow room for appeal, not because the risk is negotiable, but because trust is an integral part of the process.

Ultimately, merchant reviews and deactivations are not about enforcement for its own sake. They're about aligning the merchant base with the platform's risk appetite, regulatory obligations, and long-term integrity. A platform that enforces standards consistently builds a healthier ecosystem, one where good actors can thrive, and bad actors can't hide.

Governance for Managing Risk Across Global Markets

As a payments platform expands across borders and scales across functions, the complexity of risk doesn't just grow; it multiplies. Regulatory regimes diverge. Fraud patterns shift by market. Local partners and acquiring banks impose unique requirements. And operational teams often become fragmented across time zones, languages, and reporting lines. In this environment, risk management can no longer rely on central oversight alone. It requires governance systems designed for scale, flexibility, and cross-functional alignment.

Global risk governance begins with a clear understanding of what decisions are made locally and what must be centralized. For example, frontline teams in individual markets may manage merchant onboarding, local compliance filings, or support escalations. But policy setting, high-risk approvals, and financial reserve modeling often remain global responsibilities. Defining this split and making it explicit prevents duplication, confusion, and gaps in ownership.

To support consistency, many platforms adopt federated governance models. This means risk, legal, and compliance leads are embedded in major regional hubs, empowered to act autonomously within clearly defined limits, but closely tied to global leadership. These local leaders translate policy into practice, adapt controls for regional nuance, and surface on-the-ground insights that inform broader strategy. They function as both operators and connectors, linking the field to the center and ensuring decisions flow both ways.

Cross-functional committees often play a central role in maintaining alignment. A global risk council might meet monthly to review performance metrics, review escalated issues, and assess policy changes. Regional risk forums, meanwhile, manage more tactical coordination, aligning product, support, and operations teams within specific jurisdictions to resolve edge cases, share insights, or react to market-specific threats.

Tools and infrastructure also matter. A global governance framework requires shared systems: unified risk dashboards, standardized escalation paths, and documentation templates that allow for comparability across markets. Without these, local teams operate in isolation, making decisions that may be optimal for their region but risky at scale.

Perhaps most importantly, effective global governance requires a culture of transparency. Teams must be incentivized to flag issues early, rather than burying them due to fear of review. Risk reporting should be normalized, not stigmatized. And executive leadership must reinforce that governance is not a constraint on growth; it's what allows growth to happen sustainably and credibly.

When done well, global governance creates alignment without rigidity. It empowers teams to move quickly while staying within guardrails. It respects local expertise without compromising international standards. And it ensures that, no matter where a risk originates, the platform has a clear, coordinated, and confident way to respond.

Enterprise Risk Integration: Closing the Loop

At scale, risk cannot be managed in silos. Fraud, compliance, credit, operational gaps, and reputational exposure may each originate from different sources, but their consequences ripple across the business. That's why the goal of a mature risk program is enterprise integration: building a system where risk is not just a department or a function, but a core capability embedded into the platform's DNA.

Enterprise risk integration means more than cross-functional meetings or shared dashboards. It means aligning how risk is defined, measured, and acted upon across all teams, from engineering and product to operations, finance, legal, and leadership. It requires a shared vocabulary, clear thresholds, and common escalation paths. And it depends on systems that turn data into insight, insight into decisions, and decisions into durable action.

At the leadership level, this integration enables more effective trade-offs. Executives no longer operate in the dark or rely on anecdotal updates; they have structured reporting that connects risk signals to business outcomes. That means faster responses, more confident bets, and the ability to course-correct before problems metastasize.

At the operational level, integration creates clarity and trust. Teams know where the boundaries are, who owns what, and how to surface concerns without friction. Risk isn't something to be avoided; it's something to be understood, discussed, and designed against.

And at the strategic level, it becomes a competitive advantage. Platforms that integrate risk deeply can scale faster, enter new markets more safely, and withstand scrutiny from partners, regulators, and users with greater confidence. They don't just avoid failure; they build resilience into growth.

With the architecture now in place, spanning onboarding, transaction flows, governance, global operations, and strategic oversight, the next challenge is turning integration into adaptability. How do platforms stay ahead of emerging threats, evolving regulations, and new attack vectors? How do they continuously upgrade their defenses without slowing their momentum?

That's where we turn next: into risk evolution, and the tools, signals, and strategies that help high-growth platforms stay safe in motion.

Next, we'll explore how regulatory reporting and compliance events are managed operationally, turning obligations into repeatable, scalable processes.

Regulatory Reporting and Compliance Workflows

Ultimately, the goal of operational compliance is not just to meet expectations, but to build resilience into the business itself.

Compliance isn't just about staying out of trouble; it's about running a payments business that's sustainable, trustworthy, and respected across jurisdictions. But that only works if compliance obligations are operationalized, not just outlined in policy binders.

As platforms scale across markets and partners, the complexity of regulatory expectations increases. Authorities expect payment companies to not only implement proper controls but to demonstrate them consistently, completely, and on time. Failure to report, document, or escalate by local or international standards can quickly lead to scrutiny, sanctions, or loss of license.

That's why building a repeatable, auditable compliance workflow is essential.

Turning Rules into Processes

Each regulatory framework, whether PSD2 in Europe, AML directives in the U.S., or data privacy rules under GDPR, has its own set of reporting requirements. These might include:

➤ Suspicious Activity Reports (SARs): Triggered by AML alerts or fraud red flags.

➤ Transaction monitoring summaries: Shared with banks, regulators, or auditors.

➤ Customer due diligence records: Stored and retrieved on demand.

➤ Licensing or registration updates: Especially in money transmission or cross-border remittance

➤ Periodic compliance certifications: For PCI DSS, SOC 2, or data handling mandates

Meeting these obligations at scale means translating abstract rules into automated workflows and task ownership.

Building Operational Compliance Infrastructure

Best-in-class compliance programs are built into daily workflows, not bolted on. This means:

➢ Case management systems to track alerts, escalations, and SAR documentation.

➢ Audit trails on KYC/KYB checks, onboarding decisions, and compliance overrides.

➢ Integration with fraud and transaction monitoring tools to ensure suspicious patterns trigger a compliance review.

➢ Rule engines that trigger regulatory obligations automatically when thresholds or behaviors are met.

➢ Dashboarding and reporting tools that let teams track exposure and submission timelines across jurisdictions.

These systems not only reduce human error, but they also provide regulators with confidence that the organization takes its obligations seriously.

Human Oversight and Cross-Functional Coordination

While automation is essential, judgment matters. Many regulatory reports require interpretation. Was this merchant suspicious, or just unusual? Should a user be escalated to law enforcement or flagged internally?

To support this, leading organizations:

➢ Empower compliance analysts to review, contextualize, and finalize reports.

➢ Hold regular cross-functional reviews of open cases and regulatory trends.

➢ Include compliance leads in product and operational planning meetings.

➢ Maintain real-time documentation of decisions, escalations, and outcomes.

This creates a culture of regulatory readiness, where compliance isn't reactive; it's proactive and predictable.

Handling Regulator Interactions

No platform escapes scrutiny forever. When regulators do engage, whether through inquiries, audits, or penalties, the speed, completeness, and clarity of your response can define the outcome.

That means having:

➢ A single point of contact for each regulatory body

➢ Predefined playbooks for investigations or onsite reviews

➢ Document templates and audit folders are always up to date.

➢ Clear communication protocols between legal, ops, and leadership

Compliance workflows may not be customer-facing, but they are mission-critical. They protect licenses, partnerships, and reputation. And they enable growth, because platforms that prove they can manage risk and meet obligations are the ones that earn long-term trust.

Next, we'll examine how to maintain this operational excellence at scale, through training, tooling, and risk culture across teams.

Training, Tooling, and Risk Culture

Culture amplifies or undermines every tool and policy. When teams understand risk and are empowered to act, execution becomes seamless.

Operational risk management doesn't succeed because of tools alone; it succeeds because people understand risk, own it, and respond appropriately. As platforms scale, onboarding new team members, launching new products, and expanding into new regions, risk awareness can't remain confined to a single department. It must become part of the company's DNA.

That means investing in training, equipping teams with the right tools, and cultivating a culture where managing risk is viewed not as an obstacle, but as everyone's responsibility.

Training Beyond Compliance

Too many organizations reduce training to checklists and certifications. While baseline compliance training (e.g., AML, data handling, PCI) is necessary, it's often disconnected from the real-world scenarios teams face.

A robust risk training program goes further:

➤ Contextualized examples drawn from real cases within the business.

➤ Role-specific modules for onboarding teams, customer support, product, and engineering

➤ Simulations and live drills for fraud response, system outages, or regulatory audits

➤ Regular refreshers to stay current on emerging threats and evolving policies.

Training should be more than a formality. It should build judgment, confidence, and shared language around risk, especially at scale.

Tools That Enable Action

Risk-aware teams need more than awareness; they need access. That's where the proper tooling makes risk operational. From dashboards to alerts to action queues, systems should be built to empower teams to make fast, accurate, and auditable decisions.

Key capabilities include:

➤ Case management systems for handling escalations and investigations

➤ Real-time dashboards to monitor KRIs (Key Risk Indicators) and SLAs

➤ Risk scoring engines integrated into onboarding, transactions, and support flows.

➤ Feedback loops where manual reviews improve automated systems over time.

➤ Configurable access controls that ensure the right people have the proper visibility and decision-making authority.

These tools don't eliminate the need for human oversight; they amplify good decisions at scale.

Building and Sustaining Risk Culture

Culture is the hardest part of any operational program, and the most important. It's what turns policy into practice, and incident into improvement. A strong risk culture doesn't mean avoiding risk at all costs. It means making calculated, transparent decisions and knowing when to raise a hand.

In organizations with mature risk cultures:

➤ People feel safe reporting issues or asking questions.

➢ Product teams bring risk into planning conversations early.

➢ Compliance and risk are viewed as partners, not blockers.

➢ Mistakes are studied, not punished, and postmortems lead to improvements.

➢ Risk data is shared openly across teams, not hidden in silos.

Culture is shaped by leadership, reinforced by systems, and sustained by example. And it becomes a platform's ultimate competitive advantage, because while tools and policies can be copied, culture cannot.

Risk is operational. It touches every part of the payments ecosystem, and the only way to manage it effectively is to embed it deeply into people, processes, and products.

In the next chapter, we'll explore real-world case studies that show how these operational strategies play out in practice, highlighting what happens when risk is ignored, managed well, or turned into opportunity.

Chapter Summary: From Framework to Execution

Operationalizing risk is where theory meets pressure, and where frameworks either hold or collapse. Chapter 4 explored how payment companies bring risk management to life at scale, embedding it into the systems, workflows, and decisions that define day-to-day operations.

We began with onboarding, the critical gateway where trust is extended or denied. Effective onboarding balances speed and scrutiny, using KYC/KYB protocols, tiered risk modeling, and real-time verification to ensure that threats are filtered before they ever touch a transaction.

From there, we moved into transaction monitoring, the platform's second-by-second pulse check. Through velocity controls, behavioral analytics, and adaptive models, risk teams detect not only fraud but system abuse and customer dissatisfaction as it unfolds.

Next, we tackled the high-stakes world of disputes and chargebacks, where platforms must mediate between users and merchants without inviting fraud or damaging reputation. The right balance of automation, documentation, and proactive communication can turn disputes into early warning systems, not just cost centers.

We then examined regulatory reporting, a domain that can quietly make or break a payments company. By translating rules into workflows and building a culture of audit-readiness, leading platforms ensure that compliance doesn't lag innovation.

Finally, we looked inward at training, tooling, and culture. Because no system, no matter how sophisticated, will succeed if the people using it are disengaged, undertrained, or unsupported. When teams are empowered, risk becomes an asset. When they're uninformed, it becomes a liability.

The throughline is simple: risk management must operate at the speed of business. That means building systems that are automated but accountable, responsive but reliable, and structured enough to scale.

In the next chapter, we'll step away from theory and into the field, exploring real case studies where risk management succeeded, failed, or evolved under pressure. In payments, the most valuable lessons are often learned the hard way, but the best leaders learn them before they're repeated.

Chapter 5: Fraud Detection and Cybersecurity

No matter how robust your compliance program, how well you know your customer, or how tightly your policies are written, fraud and cyber threats remain a constant, and often invisible, presence in the payments industry. As money becomes increasingly digital and the infrastructure to move it becomes more complex, the line between criminal behavior and legitimate transactions continues to blur.

Fraud has evolved from isolated credit card theft to an industrialized, global business. Today's fraudsters are organized, well-funded, and increasingly powered by automation, artificial intelligence, and stolen data traded on dark web marketplaces. Meanwhile, cyberattacks have shifted from nuisance disruptions to existential threats. A single breach can lead to financial loss, regulatory action, customer attrition, and reputational collapse, often all at once.

The modern payment platform must be built not just for convenience and speed, but for resilience. This means detecting fraud in real time, securing systems against intrusion, and responding to incidents before they spiral out of control. It means recognizing that fraud risk and cybersecurity risk are no longer separate conversations;

they are interlinked domains that require shared intelligence, shared tooling, and shared ownership.

In this chapter, we'll explore how payment companies, from fintech startups to global processors, can build layered, intelligent defense systems that balance security with user experience. We'll examine:

➢ The most common and emerging types of payment fraud are account takeovers and synthetic identities, as well as friendly fraud and transaction laundering.

➢ The rise of real-time fraud detection is driven by machine learning, behavioral analytics, and device intelligence.

➢ The cybersecurity infrastructure is required to protect APIs, cloud systems, customer data, and internal operations from breaches and disruptions.

➢ The strategic role of incident response planning, encryption, authentication, and access control in preventing cascading failures.

➢ How cross-functional collaboration between fraud, compliance, product, and engineering teams creates faster detection and more innovative prevention.

Because in today's world, fraud is no longer about bad luck; it's about whether your defenses are ready.

Types of Payment Fraud and How They Operate

In the digital payments world, fraud doesn't come in through the front door; it slips in through the cracks. It mimics legitimate behavior, hides in trusted accounts, and evolves faster than most organizations can respond. What once looked like a stolen credit card used at a gas station now appears as a synthetic identity making peer-to-peer transfers, or a merchant laundering illegal funds through fake e-commerce orders.

Fraud today is not only more sophisticated but also designed to scale. Attackers exploit automation, social engineering, and platform vulnerabilities to launch high-volume, low-noise operations that often go undetected for weeks or months—for payment providers, understanding how these schemes work is essential to defending against them.

Let's explore some of the most common and dangerous types of payment fraud affecting the ecosystem today.

Card-Not-Present (CNP) Fraud

This is the most well-known and widely experienced form of digital payment fraud. It occurs when stolen card credentials are used to make unauthorized purchases online or over the phone, where the physical card isn't required.

CNP fraud surged during the pandemic as more commerce shifted online. Fraudsters often buy card data in bulk, including card numbers, CVVs, and billing addresses, from breaches or underground forums. They evaluate these cards on low-value transactions before moving on to higher-ticket purchases, digital goods, or gift cards that are harder to trace.

Real-world example: A fraudster purchases 10,000 stolen card numbers, uses bots to evaluate them on a gaming platform for $1 in-game credits, and identifies 400 valid cards. These are then used to buy high-end electronics for resale.

Account Takeover (ATO)

ATO fraud occurs when a fraudster gains unauthorized access to a legitimate user's account, often through phishing, credential stuffing, or SIM-swapping. Once inside, they can transfer funds, change banking details, or rack up charges using stored payment methods.

This type of fraud is hazardous because it exploits trust. To the system, it looks like the real user is acting normally, until it's too late.

Real-world example: A customer reuses their email and password across platforms. A breach at a retailer leaks that data. A fraudster logs into the customer's digital wallet, adds a new bank account, and withdraws the balance to an untraceable account, all within minutes.

Synthetic Identity Fraud

One of the fastest-growing fraud types, synthetic identity fraud involves creating entirely new identities using a mix of real and fake information. These identities often pass standard KYC checks and slowly build credibility over time, making them particularly hard to detect.

Fraudsters may apply for credit, open merchant accounts, or establish transaction histories before eventually "busting out", maxing out the system, and disappearing.

Real-world example: A fraud ring creates a fake merchant using a fabricated name, a real tax ID, and synthetic director information. They process fake transactions for months, receive payouts, then vanish just before chargebacks begin to roll in.

Friendly Fraud (First-Party Fraud)

This occurs when a legitimate user makes a purchase and then falsely disputes the charge with their card issuer, claiming fraud or non-receipt. Unlike traditional fraud, friendly fraud is initiated by the actual customer and is notoriously difficult to win in chargeback disputes.

It is particularly common in digital goods, subscription services, or industries where delivery confirmation is hard to prove.

Real-world example: A customer subscribes to a video streaming platform, watches content for several weeks, then initiates a chargeback claiming they never signed up. The issuer refunds the charge, and the platform eats the cost.

Transaction Laundering

Also known as "credit card laundering" or "factoring," this involves a legitimate-looking merchant using their account to process payments for illicit businesses. This is common in high-risk industries that cannot obtain processing accounts directly, such as counterfeit goods, unlicensed pharmaceuticals, or illegal gambling.

This fraud type poses a serious threat to acquirers and PSPs because it bypasses merchant vetting entirely and can attract regulatory action or card network penalties.

Real-world example: An online store selling "health supplements" is processing payments for an illegal sports betting site. The site embeds invisible payment links on fake pages to mask the true origin of funds.

Refund Abuse and Return Fraud

Often overlapping with friendly fraud, these schemes involve manipulating return or refund processes to obtain money or goods illegitimately. In digital platforms, this might include exploiting loopholes in payout rules or staging fake service complaints.

Real-world example: A gig worker platform offers instant payouts for completed tasks. A fraudster creates fake tasks, completes them using bot accounts, requests payouts, and cashes out before the phony nature of the work is uncovered.

Fraud is a Moving Target

Each of these fraud types represents a different attack vector, but they share a common thread: they take advantage of scale, speed, and gaps in visibility. As payments become more instantaneous and platforms more complex, fraudsters look for the soft spots, the automation gaps, the unverified behaviors, the "low friction" features that offer entry points.

Defending against them requires more than static rules. It demands intelligent, adaptive detection systems, layered defenses, and an organization-wide understanding of how fraud manifests.

In the next section, we'll explore how real-time fraud detection, powered by behavioral analytics and machine learning, helps platforms stay ahead of these evolving threats.

Real-Time Fraud Detection and Behavioral Analytics

As fraud becomes more complex, the race is no longer just to identify it; it's to identify it in real time. In the payments industry, where transactions clear in seconds and payouts can happen instantly, waiting hours (or even minutes) to flag a suspicious activity is often too late. By the time a red flag is raised, the money is gone, moved, split, or withdrawn through a web of mule accounts.

That's why leading payment platforms are shifting away from reactive, rule-based systems toward real-time, behavior-driven fraud detection, powered by machine learning and advanced analytics. These systems don't just look for known fraud patterns; they watch how customers behave, build individual profiles, and detect anomalies as they happen.

How Behavioral Analytics Works

Behavioral analytics in fraud prevention is about understanding what normal looks like and spotting what doesn't. Instead of focusing solely on complex rules like "no more than three transactions per hour," these systems analyze broader patterns:

➤ How a user typically logs in (device, location, frequency)

➤ Their historical purchase behavior (amounts, timing, categories)

➤ Typing speed, mouse movements, and navigation paths

➤ Changes in IP address, time zones, or device fingerprints

➤ Commonalities between new accounts (email domains, referral sources, shared funding methods)

If a user who transacts typically once a day suddenly initiates 25 high-value withdrawals from a new device in a foreign country, a behavioral model doesn't need a fixed rule to flag it; it detects that the behavior itself is statistically unusual.

This is the key strength of behavioral systems: they adapt to each individual or merchant, rather than applying a one-size-fits-all filter. They also learn over time, adjusting risk scores based on evolving inputs and confirmed outcomes.

The Role of Machine Learning

Machine learning (ML) takes behavioral analytics to the next level. ML models ingest massive amounts of historical data, including legitimate and fraudulent transactions, and learn to detect subtle patterns that human analysts would never see. These systems can evaluate thousands of features per transaction in milliseconds, assigning risk scores that help platforms make real-time decisions.

For example:

➢ A low score might allow a transaction to pass normally.

➢ A medium score might trigger step-up authentication (like OTP or biometric ID).

➤ A high score might block the transaction outright and flag the account for manual review.

ML models can be supervised (trained on labeled data), unsupervised (looking for natural outliers), or hybrid (combining both approaches). Many platforms also use ensemble models, multiple ML models working together, to improve accuracy and reduce false positives.

Balancing Detection and Experience

Of course, fraud detection doesn't exist in a vacuum; it must operate alongside user experience. Overzealous blocking of legitimate transactions can frustrate good customers, increase support costs, and lead to churn. That's why the best systems are not just accurate, but calibrated, using dynamic thresholds, feedback loops, and human oversight to fine-tune responses.

For example:

A first-time buyer on an e-commerce platform from a new country may be high-risk statistically, but instead of blocking them, the platform might apply a payment hold or require email confirmation.

A frequent customer making a slightly unusual purchase may be flagged, but allowed to proceed with light friction, like a CVV re-entry.

This nuanced approach, often called risk-based authentication, allows platforms to layer security in proportion to risk, preserving the flow for legitimate users while stopping bad actors in their tracks.

Integrating Fraud Intelligence Across the Platform

Modern fraud detection doesn't live in a silo. The insights generated by behavioral models and ML engines must feed into:

➢ Customer support tools (so agents understand why transactions were flagged)

➢ Compliance teams (to inform SARs or merchant reviews)

➢ Product teams (to adjust risk thresholds or improve UX for flagged users)

➢ Engineering and security teams (to track exploits, evaluate system integrity, and harden APIs)

Organizations that treat fraud detection as a cross-functional initiative, rather than an isolated toolset, are more resilient and responsive.

Seeing the Threat Before It Hits

Fraud is fast. But detection, today, can be faster. With behavioral analytics and machine learning, payment companies can move from chasing patterns to anticipating them, stopping threats not based on who committed them last time, but on how they behave this time.

In the next section, we'll shift focus to the cybersecurity infrastructure that underpins all of this, because intelligent detection is only one side of the coin. Without strong defenses, prevention is just a matter of luck.

Cybersecurity Infrastructure and Threat Prevention

While fraud detection is focused on identifying bad behavior within the transaction stream, cybersecurity is about protecting the infrastructure itself, the systems, networks, applications, and data that power every digital payment. In the payments industry, these two functions are inseparable. A breach in your cybersecurity controls doesn't just expose technical vulnerabilities; it opens the door to large-scale financial fraud, regulatory violations, and existential reputational damage.

As payments have moved online and APIs have become the connective tissue between institutions, attack surfaces have multiplied. Payment platforms today must guard against a wide range of threats: external hackers, insider threats, DDoS attacks, credential stuffing, and supply chain compromises, often all at once. In this context, cybersecurity is no longer just an IT concern. It's a core pillar of risk management, and a frontline defense in protecting the trust that payments depend on.

Securing the Foundations: Core Cyber Defenses

Cybersecurity begins with basic hygiene, but in high-stakes environments like payments, the "basics" are anything but simple.

Encryption: All sensitive data, from card numbers to passwords, must be encrypted both in transit and at rest. Platforms must ensure encryption protocols (e.g., TLS 1.2+, AES-256) are implemented across all endpoints, APIs, and storage layers. Weak or outdated cryptographic methods are not only a liability, but they're also a regulatory red flag.

Access Controls: Not every employee should have access to payment data, PII, or system configuration tools. Role-based access controls (RBAC), coupled with multi-factor authentication (MFA), ensure that even if credentials are compromised, attackers can't move freely within the system.

Network Segmentation and Firewalls: Isolating sensitive systems, such as payment gateways or settlement processors, reduces lateral movement in the event of a breach. Firewalls and intrusion prevention systems (IPS) monitor for unusual activity at the network level.

Patch Management: Zero-day vulnerabilities and unpatched software are a favorite target for attackers. Keeping infrastructure updated and having a process for rapid response to CVEs is essential.

API Security: The Payments Front Door

Modern payment platforms rely heavily on application programming interfaces (APIs), whether for merchant integrations, bank partners, or third-party services like identity verification. These APIs must be treated as critical infrastructure, not as back-end utilities.

Authentication and authorization controls must be tightly enforced. Rate limiting, IP allowlisting, and token expiration are standard defenses.

Input validation is key; attackers often inject malformed or malicious data to test boundaries and exploit weaknesses.

API abuse detection should be in place to catch bots, scraping attempts, or behavior anomalies, such as a merchant generating thousands of refund requests via script.

A single insecure API can compromise an entire platform. Some of the most significant data breaches in fintech history have stemmed not from brute-force attacks, but from poorly configured or undocumented APIs.

Defending Against External Attacks

DDoS Mitigation: Distributed denial-of-service attacks aim to overwhelm a platform's infrastructure, rendering it unusable. Payment companies should partner with CDN or anti-DDoS providers to detect and reroute malicious traffic in real time.

Credential Stuffing Protection: When attackers use previously leaked credentials to evaluate logins en-masse, detection depends on behavioral monitoring, such as device mismatches, high login velocity, or IP clustering.

Malware and Ransomware Prevention: Endpoints (especially employee laptops or customer service consoles) should be hardened against malware infections. Payment firms have been targeted by ransomware gangs that demand payment in exchange for unlocking systems or withholding stolen data from public release.

Insider Threats and Vendor Risk

Not all attacks come from the outside. Disgruntled employees, negligent contractors, or compromised partners can introduce serious vulnerabilities, especially in fast-growing fintech environments where access control is looser or less formalized.

Vendor integrations, such as KYC providers, CRM systems, or embedded finance partners, often have access to sensitive systems or data. If their defenses are weak, your exposure becomes their exposure. Third-party risk assessments, SOC 2 audits, and contractual security clauses are now a standard part of vendor onboarding and oversight.

Incident Response: Planning for the Inevitable

Even the best defenses will not stop every threat. That's why incident response planning is a critical component of payment cybersecurity. A strong response plan includes:

➢ A transparent chain of command and communication protocol

➢ Predefined steps for containment, investigation, and recovery

Regulatory notification procedures (e.g., informing data protection authorities within mandated periods)

Post-mortem reviews and control adjustments

Companies that manage breaches well often retain trust. Those who scramble, delay disclosures, or appear unprepared may suffer irreversible damage.

Cybersecurity Is Not Optional, It's Structural

In an industry built on speed, trust, and access to money, a single vulnerability can become a systemic failure. Customers expect that their data is safe. Partners assume you've locked the doors. Regulators will ask for proof.

As payment platforms scale, cybersecurity can no longer be left to chance or a single team in the basement. It must be engineered into your systems, embedded into your culture, and rehearsed like a critical business function. Because in payments, there's no such thing as a minor breach.

Next, we'll look at how these systems, fraud detection and cybersecurity, come together in the form of incident response planning and coordinated defense.

Incident Response and Recovery: When Things Go Wrong

Despite the best prevention systems, sophisticated fraud models, and hardened infrastructure, every payment company must face an uncomfortable truth: incidents will happen. Whether it's a cyber breach, a large-scale fraud attack, or a critical system outage, the question is not if, but when. What separates a catastrophic failure from a controlled event isn't luck; it's preparation.

Incident response is not about having the perfect defenses. It's about how quickly and effectively you can contain a threat, assess its impact, communicate clearly, and restore operations. In the high-speed world of digital payments, minutes matter, and disorganization can cost far more than the incident itself.

The Anatomy of an Incident

A typical payment-related incident might unfold like this: a sudden spike in refund requests is detected by the fraud team. Upon investigation, it was discovered that a merchant integration was compromised, and customer payment data was exposed. Meanwhile, customers begin reporting fraudulent charges, social media chatter escalates, and a regulator sends a request for urgent clarification.

In moments like this, the success or failure of the response hinges on preparation, clarity, and coordination. Does your team know what to do? Who owns the incident? Are there checklists, tools, and playbooks already in place? Or does chaos take over?

Key Components of an Effective Response Plan

Defined Roles and Responsibilities

Every incident needs a commander. Whether it's a fraud lead, a compliance officer, or a designated CISO, someone must be empowered to direct the response. Supporting roles, communications, engineering, legal, and customer support should be predefined and cross-trained.

Detection and Triage

Rapid detection is critical. This includes automated alerts (e.g., unusual transaction spikes, failed API calls, security logs) as well as human-reported anomalies. Once detected, incidents must be triaged based on severity: is it a minor issue or a full-blown crisis?

Containment and Remediation

The immediate goal is to stop the bleeding. That might mean deactivating affected accounts, revoking compromised API keys, pausing payment flows, or isolating systems. From there, technical teams work to identify the breach vector and remediate vulnerabilities.

Internal and External Communication

Silence can be more damaging than failure. Internally, stakeholders must be updated consistently. Externally, regulators, banking partners, and, in some cases, customers may need to be notified. This is where transparency and timing matter most. Delayed or vague communication often becomes a PR disaster.

Forensics and Documentation

While the crisis is unfolding, someone must be capturing evidence: logs, timestamps, data flow, communications, and decisions made. This documentation will be essential for post-incident review, legal protection, and regulatory reporting.

Recovery and Restoration

Restoring services requires both technical revalidation (e.g., patching, scanning, reconfiguring) and stakeholder confidence. Reopening payment rails or merchant access before confirming integrity can lead to repeat failures and increased liability.

Post-Mortem and Continuous Improvement

Every incident should conclude with a structured review: what went wrong, what went right, and how to do better next time. These learnings should be shared internally and reflected in updated training, processes, and controls.

Real-World Lessons from Payment Incidents

In 2021, a fintech suffered a platform-wide outage due to an expired TLS certificate. No backups were in place, and communication with users was delayed. The result was a 48-hour blackout and thousands of lost users, not due to the failure itself, but due to a lack of preparation and transparency.

A global PSP was fined after a breach exposed customer data. The root cause? The vendor system is insecure, with no monitoring in place. Worse, the company failed to report the breach within the 72-hour GDPR window. The technical issue was resolved in hours; the regulatory consequences lasted years.

These stories are familiar and avoidable. The organizations that fared best were not those who avoided incidents entirely, but those who were ready. Their teams practiced. Their plans were current. Their leadership communicated with honesty and speed.

From Damage Control to Institutional Resilience

Incident response isn't just a crisis discipline. It's a cultural commitment to resilience. It's the understanding that perfect prevention is a myth, but smart recovery is a reality.

For payment companies, where every second counts and trust are the currency of growth, being ready for what might go wrong is one of the most strategic advantages you can build.

In the next section, the final in this chapter, we'll explore how to unify fraud detection and cybersecurity through cross-functional collaboration and proactive defense, turning reactive response into a pre-emptive strategy.

Cross-Functional Defense: Unifying Teams, Tools, and Intelligence

Fraud detection and cybersecurity have traditionally lived in different corners of an organization, fraud under risk and operations, and cybersecurity under IT or engineering. But in the modern payments environment, that division no longer works. Threats move across boundaries. A compromised API can lead to mass account takeovers. A phishing fraud targeting customer service can open the door to merchant fraud. A delayed response from one team can undermine the efforts of another.

The future of risk management in payments doesn't belong to siloed departments; it belongs to integrated, cross-functional defense.

When teams collaborate, information flows faster. Systems integrate. Risks are spotted sooner. Customers are better protected. And perhaps most importantly, organizations gain the agility to respond in real time, not just to fraud, but to the shifting tactics of attackers, the evolving demands of regulators, and the changing behaviors of users.

The Case for Integration

Let's say your fraud team notices a spike in refund requests linked to a particular IP address. They flag it as potential abuse. However, they are unaware that the IP also triggered dozens of failed login attempts across the platform earlier that day, due to their lack of access to system logs. That data lives with the cybersecurity team.

Now imagine the two teams are connected. That IP flag becomes part of a shared alert. The fraud team can investigate with context. The security team can add the IP to a blocklist. The support team can be alerted to verify affected users. That's intelligence in action, not in isolation.

Breaking Down the Silos

A unified defense requires more than good intentions. It requires intentional structure:

Shared Platforms: Fraud tools, SIEM systems, and case management dashboards all should feed into a central hub where patterns can be correlated. This gives teams a single source of truth, rather than scattered spreadsheets or conflicting alerts.

Joint Response Protocols: Incidents should be triaged by a multi-disciplinary team, including fraud, security, compliance, legal, and engineering, each bringing their lens to the problem. This leads to faster containment and more robust decision-making.

Regular Intelligence Sharing: Through weekly or monthly risk syncs, teams share trends, suspicious behavior, new fraud methods, and attack attempts, ensuring that institutional knowledge spreads horizontally, not just upward.

Cross-Training and Shadowing: Fraud analysts should understand basic cybersecurity principles. Security engineers should be familiar with fraud models. Support agents should be trained to recognize social engineering red flags.

Leadership Support: True integration starts at the top. When executives see risk as a shared responsibility, not a cost center, they allocate resources to integration, not isolation.

The Benefits of Unified Risk Intelligence

When teams work together:

➢ Response times shrink.

➢ False positives decrease.

➢ Risk decisions become more contextualized.

➢ Trust is built across the organization.

It's not just about stopping attacks. It's about anticipating them, learning from them, and evolving as fast as your adversaries do.

Turning Reactive into Proactive

The convergence of fraud and cybersecurity is not a trend; it's an inevitability. In the high-speed world of digital payments, risk doesn't respect departmental lines. The platforms that endure will be those that break down silos, invest in shared infrastructure, and build a culture of collaboration around threat defense.

Because in the end, defending your platform isn't a job for one team, it's a mission for everyone.

Chapter Summary: Staying Ahead of the Threat

Fraud and cybersecurity risks are the twin specters of the modern payments industry, invisible until they strike, and often devastating when they do. As we've explored throughout this chapter, today's threats are faster, wiser, and more interconnected than ever before. But so are the tools, the intelligence, and the strategies available to fight them.

We began by understanding how payment fraud has evolved. From simple card-not-present theft to synthetic identities and sophisticated laundering schemes, modern fraud is industrialized. It exploits automation, weak signals, and fragmented defenses to siphon off value quietly. Recognizing the tactics behind account takeovers, friendly fraud, and transaction laundering isn't just about loss prevention; it's about protecting the very systems that move global money.

We then looked at how platforms are fighting back in real time. Behavioral analytics and machine learning have changed the game, allowing payment companies to move from reactive fraud filters to dynamic, adaptive risk scoring. These tools analyze how people behave, not just what they do, and allow for nuanced, real-time interventions that stop bad actors without alienating good users.

But technology alone isn't enough. We shifted focus to the foundational infrastructure that underpins security: encryption, access controls, API protections, and network segmentation. In a world of open systems and constant integrations, defending your architecture is non-negotiable. Cyber threats are not abstract risks; they are business-ending events when managed poorly.

And when things do go wrong, because they will, incident response becomes the difference between a bad day and a crisis. We explored how preparation, communication, and coordinated recovery can limit the impact of a breach or fraud event. A solid plan, evaluated and owned across departments, doesn't just reduce damage; it builds trust, internally and externally.

Finally, we brought it all together by emphasizing the need for cross-functional collaboration. In a connected ecosystem, risk is no longer the sole domain of fraud analysts or IT teams. When fraud, cybersecurity, compliance, and engineering teams work in isolation, cracks appear. But when they unite, with shared systems, intelligence, and purpose, those cracks become seams of strength.

At its core, this chapter reinforces an urgent but straightforward truth: resilience in payments isn't just about defense, it's about readiness. The companies that endure aren't the ones that eliminate all threats, but the ones that anticipate, adapt, and recover fast.

In Chapter 6, we'll take that mindset global, exploring how risk management becomes even more complex in the realm of cross-border payments, where regulatory fragmentation, currency volatility, and geopolitical pressure create new layers of exposure. Because as payments scale across borders, so must our risk strategy.

Section 3: Practical Applications

Chapter 6: Risk in Cross-Border Payments

Moving money across borders is one of the most powerful capabilities of the modern payments industry, and one of its most complex. Cross-border transactions open doors to global commerce, financial inclusion, and economic growth. But behind every international transfer lies a web of risk far more intricate than what domestic payment systems face.

Unlike domestic payments, which operate under a single set of rules, currency, and regulators, cross-border payments traverse multiple legal systems, financial infrastructures, currencies, and compliance regimes. Each layer introduces friction. Each area introduces uncertainty. And every participant, from correspondent banks and currency exchanges to processors and platforms, adds a potential point of failure or exposure.

The result is a space where operational risk, compliance risk, liquidity risk, and even geopolitical risk converge.

For example, a payment from a freelancer in the Philippines to a client in Germany might seem simple on the surface. But behind the scenes, that transaction may pass through four banks, two currency exchanges, three regulatory frameworks, a sanctions screening layer, and an FX conversion, all before the money clears. If any single link breaks, due to regulation, a technical glitch, or policy conflict, the entire transaction is delayed, lost, or rejected.

In this chapter, we'll examine:

➢ The unique risk exposures that emerge in cross-border payments include currency volatility, settlement delays, de-risking, and AML mismatches.

➢ The challenges of regulatory fragmentation and why even well-meaning platforms can fall afoul of foreign compliance regimes.

➢ The risk trade-offs in various cross-border models, from SWIFT corridors to blockchain rails to e-wallet interoperability, are significant.

➢ How to design a cross-border risk strategy that accounts for regional complexity, partner dependencies, and end-user trust.

Cross-border payments offer tremendous business opportunities, but without strong risk management, they can become a minefield. This chapter is about navigating that minefield with clarity, agility, and global awareness.

Because when money moves across borders, so do the risks and the responsibilities.

Currency Risk and Liquidity Challenges

At the heart of every cross-border payment lies a simple truth: money must change form. A U.S. customer paying a supplier in India, or a German buyer purchasing from a seller in Brazil, must move funds not only across geographies, but also across currencies. And that transformation introduces one of the most fundamental challenges in international payments: currency risk.

Currency risk, also known as foreign exchange (FX) risk, refers to the potential for financial loss due to fluctuations in exchange rates. In a global economy where exchange rates can shift dramatically by the hour (or even the second), this risk isn't just theoretical. It affects pricing, profit margins, settlement values, and even customer satisfaction.

The Mechanics of FX Exposure

Let's say a U.K.-based fintech offers cross-border payouts to freelancers in Kenya, paying out in Kenyan Shillings (KES). The platform receives funds in GBP from its clients, holds a balance in USD with a correspondent bank, and settles locally in KES. That payment flow crosses three currencies, three liquidity pools, and at least two FX conversions, each vulnerable to rate movement.

If the GBP weakens against the KES between the time of the customer transaction and the platform's actual conversion, the payout may become more expensive than anticipated. If the platform absorbs those costs, it eats into margins. If passed on to the customer, it risks dissatisfaction or reputational loss.

And this isn't limited to exotic currencies. Even mainstream corridors like USD-EUR or USD-INR experience volatility. In 2022 alone, the U.S. dollar rose and fell sharply against major currencies, driven by inflation, central bank policy, and geopolitical events. Companies without hedging or real-time FX controls found themselves paying more, or receiving less, than expected.

Liquidity Management in a Multi-Currency World

Currency risk is tightly coupled with another significant challenge: liquidity management. For a payment provider to offer instant or near-instant cross-border payouts, it needs to have pre-funded liquidity pools in multiple currencies, often held in local bank accounts or via partner institutions.

But tying up capital across 10 or 20 countries is expensive. Balances must be topped up based on transaction volume forecasts, and idle funds erode efficiency. Worse still, liquidity mismatches can delay transactions. If a platform runs out of PHP liquidity in the Philippines during a holiday weekend, for example, customer payments could be postponed until funding resumes, a costly and reputationally risky failure.

Managing this liquidity requires a blend of:

➢ Cash flow forecasting across currencies and markets.

➢ Intraday reconciliation of balances and settlements

➢ Real-time FX execution, sometimes through aggregators or in-house trading desks

➢ Partnerships with local banks or e-wallet providers that can offer just-in-time liquidity or overdraft capabilities.

For smaller fintechs and remittance platforms, the lack of access to affordable and reliable liquidity partners can be a significant growth barrier and one of the most acute risks when scaling internationally.

Mitigating Currency and Liquidity Risks

Some organizations implement hedging strategies, using forward contracts or currency options to lock in FX rates and reduce exposure. Others rely on dynamic FX pricing, where the cost of currency conversion is passed to the customer in real time, based on market conditions, a model used widely by neobanks and FX platforms like Wise or Revolut.

More sophisticated platforms use real-time routing to direct payments through corridors that offer the best liquidity and lowest volatility at a given moment. This requires deep integration with banking APIs, FX providers, and settlement networks, but provides more control and stability.

Finally, having clear policies on FX margins, customer transparency, and error recovery is essential. When currency swings result in an underpayment or a failed conversion, customers expect a fast, fair resolution, and regulators often expect disclosures.

The High Cost of Movement

In cross-border payments, moving money is not the same as moving value. Without careful currency and liquidity planning, even a perfectly executed transaction can result in financial, reputational, or both losses.

This is why payment providers must treat FX not as a backend function, but as a core component of the risk framework. From pricing models to treasury operations, every decision should reflect the reality that currencies move, and you need to move with them.

Next, we'll explore how the regulatory fragmentation of global jurisdictions introduces a second, equally complex challenge: navigating legal and compliance risks when payments cross borders.

Regulatory Fragmentation and Compliance Risks

Cross-border payments don't just move money; they move through a mosaic of legal systems, regulatory bodies, and enforcement frameworks. Every country, and in many cases every region within a country, has its own rules governing who can send and receive funds, how those funds must be documented, and what obligations payment platforms have in the process.

Unlike domestic payments, where a single regulator typically governs operations (such as FINTRAC in Canada or the FCA in the U.K.), cross-border payments face regulatory fragmentation, a patchwork of sometimes complementary, sometimes conflicting rules. For payment providers, this creates one of the most persistent and high-stakes categories of risk: compliance exposure in foreign jurisdictions.

The Complexity of Multi-Jurisdiction Compliance

Let's imagine a fintech headquartered in Singapore, offering remittance services to migrant workers in the Middle East and Southeast Asia. To operate legally and compliantly, it may need:

➤ A license from Singapore's Monetary Authority of Singapore (MAS)

➤ Registration with the Central Bank of the Philippines (BSP) to disburse funds locally.

➤ A partnership with a licensed intermediary in the UAE to manage inbound payments.

➤ Compliance with the EU General Data Protection Regulation (GDPR) if any users are based in Europe.

➤ Adherence to U.S. OFAC sanctions rules if it processes any U.S. dollar-denominated transactions.

Each of these requirements comes with its documentation standards, reporting obligations, transaction limits, and enforcement risks. Missing just one, say, failing to report a suspicious transaction in a district with mandatory SAR filing, can result in regulatory sanctions, de-banking, or worse.

Common Regulatory Risks in Cross-Border Payments

Licensing Gaps: Many countries require foreign payment service providers to obtain local authorization or operate through a licensed partner. Companies that expand rapidly without securing the proper permissions risk being labeled as operating illegally, even unintentionally.

AML/KYC Misalignment: Standards for KYC and AML differ widely. A platform may meet its home country's requirements but fall short in a destination country with stricter rules, such as enhanced due diligence for high-risk customers or politically exposed persons (PEPs).

Sanctions Compliance: International payments often involve multiple intermediaries and currencies. A single link to a sanctioned entity, even if indirect, can trigger enforcement actions, especially when U.S. dollar clearing is engaged.

Data Privacy Conflicts: The transfer of personal and financial data across borders may violate local data sovereignty laws, such as Brazil's LGPD or India's proposed Digital Personal Data Protection Act. Regulators increasingly demand local data storage and processing, adding operational and legal complexity.

Currency Controls and Capital Restrictions: Some countries impose restrictions on outbound capital flows or mandate central bank approvals for currency conversion. Non-compliance can result in blocked payments, frozen funds, or penalties.

De-Risking and Loss of Access

Perhaps the most damaging outcome of regulatory non-compliance is de-risking, when banks or partners sever relationships with platforms they view as too risky or burdensome to maintain. In recent years, many global banks have closed accounts or terminated services for remittance firms, crypto exchanges, and high-risk PSPs simply because the perceived regulatory exposure outweighed the business benefit.

When a platform is de-banked, it may lose the ability to settle funds, process transactions, or access correspondent networks, effectively shutting down operations overnight. And re-establishing those relationships can take months, if not years.

Building a Cross-Border Compliance Framework

To operate safely across borders, payment companies must:

➤ Map local laws and licensing requirements in every market they enter.

➤ Standardize AML/KYC policies while layering in regional customizations.

➤ Maintain strong vendor due diligence, mainly when relying on third-party partners for local compliance.

➤ Implement global sanctions screening with multi-district list coverage and real-time updates.

➤ Invest in regulatory technology (RegTech) that supports document tracking, reporting, audit trails, and policy management.

Just as importantly, they must cultivate relationships with local regulators and banking partners, staying informed about upcoming legal changes and demonstrating their commitment to proactive compliance.

A Global Business Requires Global Awareness

In cross-border payments, ignorance is not a defense, and inconsistency is not tolerated for long. Regulatory fragmentation may be one of the most frustrating aspects of global finance. Still, it is also one of the most navigable, with the right strategy, the right tools, and a culture of compliance woven into the business model.

Because the goal isn't just to move money across borders, it's to do so legally, securely, and sustainably.

Next, we'll examine another risk dimension specific to cross-border payments: Geopolitical and Sanctions Risk, where global tensions become operational threats.

Geopolitical and Sanctions Risk

Cross-border payments don't just move through economic channels; they move through the currents of global politics. In an increasingly volatile world, geopolitical tensions and sanctions regimes have become potent disruptors of financial flows. For payment providers, these forces represent a uniquely challenging category of risk: one that is essentially outside their control yet directly affects their operations.

Geopolitical risk refers to the impact that international conflicts, diplomatic breakdowns, or political instability can have on financial systems. Sanctions risk, often a byproduct of geopolitics, refers to the legal exposure companies face when doing business with blocked individuals, organizations, or entire countries.

Together, they create a landscape where a transaction that's legal today may become illegal tomorrow, and where a sudden policy shift in one country can freeze millions of dollars in motion.

How Geopolitics Affects Payment Flows

Consider a European remittance company serving the Ukrainian diaspora. In early 2022, what had been a stable and profitable corridor suddenly became a high-risk zone overnight due to the Russian invasion. Banking relationships were disrupted. Currency values plummeted. Regulatory guidance shifted. Transaction monitoring thresholds tightened. Cross-border settlements that previously took hours now faced days of delays or total breakdown.

This isn't an isolated scenario. Around the world, payment companies are grappling with:

Unstable regimes where sudden coups or civil unrest trigger account freezes and capital flight.

Diplomatic breakdowns where previously trusted banking corridors become inaccessible due to conflict.

Trade sanctions that make it illegal to process payments to or from specific individuals, industries, or financial institutions.

The 2022 sanctions against Russia are a clear example of how quickly geopolitics can upend financial operations. Dozens of Russian banks were cut off from the SWIFT network. U.S. and EU sanctions blocked hundreds of entities. Platforms with even indirect exposure, such as facilitating payroll or FX for companies with Russian clients, had to scramble to identify, isolate, and reroute affected funds.

Understanding Sanctions Risk in Practice

Sanctions are imposed by governments and international bodies, such as the U.S. (OFAC), EU, UN, UK (OFSI), and others, and they can apply to:

➢ Individuals (e.g., politically exposed persons or alleged criminals)

➢ Companies or institutions (e.g., banks, oil companies)

➢ Countries or regions (e.g., North Korea, Iran, Crimea)

➢ Violating sanctions, even unintentionally, can result in:

➢ Massive fines (sometimes exceeding tens of millions of dollars)

➢ Reputational damage that erodes partner trust

➢ Loss of banking relationships or de-risking

Criminal charges in cases of willful negligence

What makes sanctions especially complex is their jurisdictional reach. A fintech based in Canada that processes USD transactions may still fall under U.S. OFAC district, even if no American customers are involved. A European PSP that allows customers to use crypto to pay a sanctioned entity, even unknowingly, may be in breach of international law.

Managing Geopolitical and Sanctions Risk

Unlike fraud or compliance risk, geopolitical and sanctions risks can't always be predicted. But they can be prepared for.

Innovative payment providers take proactive steps to:

> ➤ Continuously update sanctions lists across jurisdictions, including watchlists for secondary sanctions and export controls.

> ➤ Geofence transactions or apply enhanced screening in high-risk corridors.

> ➤ Develop flexible routing logic that enables payments to transition away from high-risk institutions or networks as tensions escalate.

> ➤ Conduct periodic geopolitical risk assessments across their most active markets, flagging countries with high volatility or a history of policy swings.

> ➤ Maintain legal and regulatory advisors who monitor sanctions trends and interpret gray areas.

In high-risk regions, it's also essential to implement manual review and escalation protocols, especially when transactions involve large sums, politically exposed persons, or industries frequently associated with illicit finance (e.g., arms, energy, mining).

Navigating the Unpredictable

Geopolitical and sanctions risk sits at the intersection of compliance, legal, reputational, and operational exposure. It is one of the few risks that can instantly halt a business line, not because of fraud or failure, but because the rules of engagement have changed.

To operate globally, payment providers must be agile enough to respond and compliant enough to adapt, because the world will keep shifting, and your systems must change with it.

In the next and final section of this chapter, we'll explore how to bring it all together by designing a cross-border risk strategy that is proactive, scalable, and resilient in the face of complexity.

Designing a Proactive Cross-Border Risk Strategy

By now, the picture is clear: cross-border payments are rich in opportunity but steeped in complexity. Between currency volatility, fragmented regulation, sanctions exposure, and operational dependency on third-party rails, the risks don't just increase with international expansion; they multiply.

And yet, global reach remains a core goal for nearly every payment platform. The key to achieving it sustainably lies in strategy, not reaction. A proactive cross-border risk approach is not about trying to eliminate every threat. It's about building systems, structures, and processes that allow a business to scale globally while staying agile, compliant, and resilient.

This begins with understanding that cross-border risk is not one function's job. It's not just compliance, or legal, or treasury. It's a shared framework that connects product, partnerships, operations, and executive leadership. The businesses that get this right are the ones that weave risk awareness into every global decision they make, from launching new corridors to onboarding foreign merchants to selecting local banking partners.

A proactive strategy starts with mapping exposure across the entire transaction lifecycle. Where does FX risk lie? Which partners are critical to settlement? Are your KYC and AML policies sufficient for each region you serve? How fast can you respond if a regulator changes course or a sanctions list is updated overnight?

The strongest organizations conduct scenario planning and stress testing regularly, simulating disruptions like a currency crash, a de-banking event, or a sudden license restriction. These exercises are not just academic. They prepare internal teams to move quickly and confidently when the real-world equivalent unfolds, and in cross-border payments, it inevitably will.

Another vital element of a robust strategy is partner diligence and diversification. Relying on a single local bank, FX provider, or payment rail can be efficient in the short term, but it introduces fragility. Platforms that build optionality, by maintaining relationships with multiple providers in key markets, gain a critical layer of redundancy that protects against outages, political shifts, or sudden partner failures.

Technology also plays a central role. A well-architected system can flag jurisdiction-specific risks, enforce localized compliance checks, and reroute transactions through lower-risk corridors automatically. But this technology must be designed with flexibility in mind; hardcoding for today's rules often breaks under tomorrow's realities.

Perhaps most importantly, a proactive cross-border risk strategy requires governance. This doesn't mean bloated committees or endless policy reviews. It means clearly defined roles, regular alignment between business and compliance teams, and executive accountability. When risk is owned at the top, the rest of the organization follows suit, and risk decisions become part of product and growth planning, not an afterthought.

From Complexity to Control

Cross-border risk can feel overwhelming, especially when managed piecemeal. But when approached strategically, it becomes manageable. Predictable. Even advantageous.

Companies that understand global risk are not only better protected, but they're also better positioned to earn trust from regulators, banks, investors, and users. They become the platforms that survive shocks, grow through uncertainty, and lead in markets where others hesitate.

In Chapter 7, we'll shift focus from external threats to internal resilience, exploring how culture, training, and governance shape the foundation of a payment company's long-term risk maturity.

Chapter 7: Culture and Governance

Technology can catch anomalies. Policies can define boundaries. Tools can stop fraud and flag violations. But none of it works if the people behind the systems don't believe in, or understand, their role in risk management. This is where many payment companies struggle, especially during periods of rapid growth. They build strong technical defenses but fail to create a culture that supports them.

Risk management isn't just a system of controls; it's a way of thinking. It's how a customer support agent manages a suspicious refund request. The question is whether a junior engineer speaks up before deploying a change without QA. The question is whether someone in business development knows not to push through a high-risk merchant just to hit a quarterly number. These are cultural decisions, not technical ones, and they make the difference between companies that spot risks early and those that discover them too late.

Culture is what happens when no one is watching. And in the world of payments, where high-velocity decisions are made every minute, a strong culture of risk awareness isn't a nice-to-have; it's non-negotiable.

In this chapter, we'll explore:

➢ How risk culture is shaped by leadership and incentives

➢ The importance of clear governance structures that define ownership and escalation paths.

➢ Why training and awareness programs must evolve alongside threats.

➢ And how to balance innovation and speed with responsibility and accountability, especially in high-growth environments

Ultimately, we'll show that sustainable risk management isn't just about rules and software. It's about people. And the organizations that understand this are the ones best equipped to navigate whatever comes next.

Leadership, Accountability, and Risk Ownership

At the core of every resilient payments company is one unshakable truth: risk culture starts at the top. You can write all the policies you want, but if leadership doesn't visibly support, prioritize, and embody risk awareness, no one else in the organization will either. Risk tolerance isn't just a line in a document; it's revealed through daily decisions, incentives, and the tone leaders set in boardrooms, Slack channels, and product reviews.

Too often, especially in fast-moving fintechs, risk is treated like an afterthought, a downstream team that "handles issues" after the fact. In these environments, the product pushes forward while compliance lags. Growth is prioritized while risk is rationalized. Teams operate in silos, and ownership becomes blurry. When something goes wrong, the question isn't just "what happened?", it's "who was responsible?" And often, no one knows.

That's where governance and accountability come in.

Making Risk Everyone's Responsibility, But No One's Confusion

Transparent governance doesn't mean spreading risk so thin that no one owns it. It means defining who is responsible for what and empowering those people to act.

The C-suite must understand and champion the organization's risk appetite, not just sign off on it.

The board must receive regular, honest reporting on emerging risks, control gaps, and significant exposures, and be prepared to challenge assumptions.

Product teams should be aware of the compliance thresholds applicable to their launches and have a role in determining how controls are implemented, ensuring they do not hinder innovation.

Engineering teams should be part of incident response plans, security reviews, and access management audits, not just building features in a vacuum.

Customer service must be trained to detect red flags and know how (and where) to escalate them.

Ownership doesn't just reduce failure; it accelerates response. When a suspicious pattern emerges or a rule is bypassed, everyone should know who's on point. Not after the incident, before it ever begins.

Leadership's Role in Modeling Behavior

Leaders don't need to be compliance experts, but they must be risk-aware decision-makers. When executives cut corners, override controls, or ignore uncomfortable truths in pursuit of growth, that message echoes down the chain. Culture becomes not what's written in onboarding slides, but what's tolerated in performance reviews and celebrated in team meetings.

Authentic leadership in risk means:

➤ Being transparent about trade-offs and mistakes.

➤ Rewarding escalation when people spot issues, not punishing them.

> ➤ Creating space in roadmaps and budgets for risk reviews, not just growth metrics.

And perhaps most importantly, it means not waiting for regulators or customers to force action. Proactive leadership builds resilience. Reactive leadership patches holes.

Risk Ownership Is Strategic Ownership

Ultimately, embedding risk into leadership and accountability isn't about slowing the business down; it's about making it more durable. Payment companies that understand who owns risk at every level and empower those owners to act can move faster with more confidence.

Because in payments, it's not just about moving money, it's about making sure that when something breaks, someone's there who knows exactly what to do.

Training, Awareness, and a Culture of Escalation

Even the best governance framework will fail if the people within it don't know how to recognize risk, or don't feel empowered to speak up when they do. In payments, where threats evolve quickly and operational blind spots can lead to systemic failures, the difference between resilience and crisis often comes down to one moment:

does someone notice something and say something before it's too late?

That moment is shaped not by policy, but by culture.

Creating a risk-aware culture isn't about fear or restriction. It's about confidence and clarity. People need to know what to look for, how to act, and who to tell. That starts with training, but it doesn't stop there.

From Checkbox Training to Embedded Learning

In too many companies, risk training is treated as a once-a-year compliance exercise. Employees click through e-learning modules, pass a short quiz, and move on, forgetting most of it within hours. These programs check boxes but do little to build fundamental awareness.

By contrast, in companies with strong risk cultures, training is:

➢ Role-specific, tailored to what risk looks like in each department.

➢ Contextual, using real examples from the business, not generic case studies.

➢ Ongoing, reinforced through regular touchpoints, not just annual refreshers.

> ➤ Interactive, encouraging participation, feedback, and discussion.

For instance, support teams might receive training on how social engineering attacks unfold, with redacted chat logs from real cases. Engineers might walk through postmortems of outages caused by overlooked access controls. Sales teams might review warning signs for high-risk merchants, not to scare them, but to help them avoid downstream fallout.

The Power of Escalation, and Why It Fails Without Trust

Even when employees recognize a problem, escalation doesn't always happen. Often, it's because people:

> ➤ Don't want to be the one who slows things down.

> ➤ Don't feel confident that their concern is valid.

> ➤ Don't know who to go to.

> ➤ Worry that it might reflect poorly on their performance.

That's why psychological safety is as important as policy. Organizations must make it explicitly clear, in both words and actions, which raising a concern is a sign of strength, not weakness.

This begins with how leaders respond to escalations. When someone flags a possible vulnerability, is the response "we'll look into it later," or "thank you, let's dig into this now"? When someone spots a merchant who looks suspicious, are they brushed off for overreacting, or looped into a follow-up with risk and compliance?

Every reaction either reinforces a culture of escalation or discourages it.

Making Escalation Easy, Not Bureaucratic

In high-functioning payments companies, escalation is a process, not a power struggle. There are clear channels, including a Slack channel, a form, and direct contact, as well as follow-through mechanisms. Escalations are acknowledged, tracked, and reviewed. Even when they turn out to be false alarms, they are treated with respect.

Some organizations formalize this through programs like:

➤ "Risk Champions" in each department who function as escalation conduits.

➢   Monthly "Red Flag Reviews" where team members discuss close calls or concerns.

➢   Internal newsletters highlight recent incidents, what was learned, and how it was managed.

The result? Everyone starts thinking like a risk owner, even if risk isn't in their job title.

Building Everyday Vigilance

Risk training and escalation aren't emergency tools; they're part of the day-to-day rhythm of responsible operations. In a world where a single overlooked misstep can lead to fraud, fines, or reputational fallout, culture is the real control system.

Because when everyone is trained, empowered, and trusted to act, risk stops being a hidden danger and becomes a shared responsibility.

Balancing Innovation, Speed, and Risk Discipline

In payments, innovation isn't optional; it's survival. The industry rewards speed: faster onboarding, instant payouts, one-click checkout, embedded finance, borderless wallets. The pressure to launch quickly and scale aggressively is real, especially for fintechs and disruptors. But speed without structure is a risk multiplier, not a growth strategy.

The tension between innovation and risk management is one of the most critical balancing acts a modern payments company must master. When innovation runs unchecked, you get fragile systems, overlooked fraud vectors, and regulatory blind spots. When risk management becomes overly rigid, product velocity suffers, customer experience degrades, and the company loses its competitive edge.

The solution isn't choosing between them; it's learning to integrate risk into the pace of innovation.

The Myth of the Risk Roadblock

Too often, risk and compliance teams are perceived as bottlenecks, the departments that say "no." The product team wants to ship a new feature, but compliance requires another round of reviews. Engineering wants to cut a release; risk wants another test. Business development wants to onboard a major merchant, but the fraud team throws a red flag.

But in high-performing companies, risk teams aren't blockers; they're strategic partners. The earlier they're involved, the fewer surprises arise downstream. When risk is embedded in the build cycle, reviews become lighter, not heavier. Escalations become faster, not slower. And risk trade-offs become deliberate, not accidental.

Building Risk into the Development Lifecycle

➤ This integration begins with culture but is rooted in process. Mature organizations build risk-aware product development frameworks where every new feature or market launch passes through the right lenses:

➤ What could go wrong?

➤ How could this be exploited?

➤ What new obligations does this create?

➤ What controls should be embedded from day one?

For example, launching a new payout API isn't just an engineering story; it's a risk story. Who can access it? How is rate limiting enforced? What KYC tier is required to use it? How are failed disbursements managed? The earlier these questions are asked, the less friction there is at launch, and the less risk of rework or retroactive fixes under regulatory pressure.

When risk thinking is built into product design, you don't slow down innovation; you reduce the number of times you have to hit the brakes.

Managing Risk Appetite in a High-Velocity Environment

Of course, not all risks can be eliminated, nor should they be. Growth inherently involves risk. New products, markets, and business models come with uncertainty. The goal is not to create a zero-risk company (which doesn't exist), but to make sure that risks are taken with eyes wide open.

This is where clearly defined risk appetite, set at the leadership level, becomes a guiding compass. Teams should know which types of risk are acceptable in pursuit of innovation, and which are deal-breakers. For example:

➤ A modest uptick in chargeback ratios for a new merchant category may be acceptable.

➤ A lapse in PCI compliance during a busy product sprint is not.

By clearly drawing those lines, teams are empowered to make decisions quickly, not by avoiding risk, but by understanding it.

Innovating with Confidence, Not Recklessness

The fastest companies are not those that ignore risk; they're the ones who design for it, plan around it, and recover from it gracefully. When risk and speed are aligned, innovation becomes safer, more sustainable, and ultimately more successful.

Because in the payments industry, it's not just about how fast you can launch, it's about how well you can last.

Embedding Risk Culture Across the Organization

Culture isn't a slogan. It's not a slide deck, a handbook, or a poster on the wall. It's how people behave when no one is watching. And in the world of payments, where mistakes are expensive, regulations are complex, and attackers are relentless, your culture is your first and last line of defense.

Embedding a culture of risk doesn't happen overnight. It's built through leadership behavior, team rituals, incentive structures, and the systems that support decision-making. Most importantly, it's embedded through consistency. Not just in how you respond to major incidents, but in how you manage the day-to-day gray areas: the edge cases, the trade-offs, the internal debates that never make headlines, but define who you are as a company.

In strong organizations, risk awareness becomes ambient. People don't need to ask whether a transaction looks suspicious; they raise it instinctively. Teams don't wait until after launch to ask if something needs compliance approval; it's part of the planning process. Engineers don't see security as someone else's job; they build for it. Business teams don't cut corners on merchant due diligence; they see it as protecting the brand they're growing.

Making Risk a Shared Language

One of the most effective ways to embed culture is to provide teams with a shared language around risk. This includes:

➢ Clear, standard definitions of risk categories.

➢ Open conversations about trade-offs, what's acceptable and what's not.

➢ Transparency about incidents and lessons learned.

➢ Leadership involves modeling the correct behavior when mistakes happen.

A team that talks about risk openly is a team that learns from it. When escalations are normalized, near-misses are shared, and cross-functional reviews are welcomed, culture reinforces itself. New hires absorb it. Existing teams amplify it. And over time, it becomes a competitive advantage.

Sustaining Culture Through Growth and Change

Maintaining a strong risk culture becomes harder as a company scales. New regions bring new threats. New hires bring different habits. Mergers, pivots, and leadership changes can dilute what was once clear. That's why culture must be intentional and protected.

This means:

➢ Regularly refreshing training and onboarding to reflect real-world threats.

➢ Rotating risk champions across teams to ensure broad ownership.

➢ Ensuring risk is part of performance metrics and team OKRs.

➢ Conducting cultural health checks, not just compliance audits.

A fast-growing payments company with thousands of employees across continents can't rely on gut instinct to maintain its culture. It needs systems, rituals, and reinforcement mechanisms to keep risk top-of-mind, even as the business moves forward at full speed.

Culture as Infrastructure

At its best, culture becomes invisible infrastructure, the unspoken protocols that guide decisions, shape habits, and prevent catastrophe before it starts. It reduces the cost of oversight, increases the speed of alignment, and ensures that when things go wrong, you recover stronger.

A resilient risk culture doesn't prevent all problems. But it ensures that your company sees them sooner, responds faster, and learns better.

Because in payments, where the margin for error is razor-thin, culture isn't a soft asset; it's the hardest one to build, and the hardest one to fake.

Chapter Summary

Throughout this chapter, we've explored a truth that many companies learn too late: tools and policies don't manage risk, people do. Culture, more than any system or framework, is what determines how effectively a payments organization identifies, responds to, and recovers from threats.

Risk culture begins with leadership. When executives prioritize integrity over expediency and reward thoughtful escalation over silence, they lay the groundwork for an organization that values vigilance. Without this tone from the top, even the most sophisticated compliance structures collapse under the weight of indifference or denial.

We saw how accountability and governance aren't about creating bureaucracy; they're about clarity. When risk ownership is clearly defined and embedded across departments, decisions are made faster, with greater confidence and fewer blind spots. Risk becomes a shared responsibility, not a game of deflection.

Training, we learned, must go far beyond the checkbox. The companies that thrive are those where every team understands what risk looks like in their specific context and feels safe enough to call it out. Creating a culture of escalation isn't about paranoia. It's about empowering everyone to protect the platform.

Innovation and risk may seem like opposing forces, but we reframed them as co-pilots. When risk is brought into the development lifecycle early, constructively, and continuously, it supports speed rather than suppressing it. Guardrails don't slow you down when they're part of the track.

And finally, we recognized that culture is not a side effect; it is a strategic asset. When risk thinking becomes ambient, when teams speak a common language, and when escalation is normalized, an organization becomes not only safer, but it becomes stronger. More cohesive. More adaptive. More prepared for what's next.

In the next chapter, we'll apply this cultural lens to a critical operational frontier: third-party risk management. Because in payments, it's not just your controls that matter, it's the people and platforms you rely on, and whether their standards can stand up to yours.

Chapter 8: Third-Party Risk in the Supply Chain

No payment company operates alone. Whether you're a fintech startup, a global acquirer, or a B2B wallet provider, your ability to deliver fast, secure, and compliant services depends on a network of third parties behind the scenes. These include card networks, issuing and acquiring banks, KYC providers, cloud infrastructure, fraud detection vendors, payout partners, payment gateways, white-label platforms, and beyond.

This intricate web, often referred to as the payments supply chain, creates immense value. It enables companies to scale quickly, enter new markets, and leverage best-in-class capabilities without building everything in-house. But it also makes a layered and sometimes opaque risk profile. When you outsource a function, you don't outsource responsibility.

Every third-party relationship introduces potential points of failure: technical, financial, reputational, and regulatory. A KYC vendor with outdated sanctions data could expose you to fines. A processor experiencing downtime during a peak sales event could damage your reputation. A cloud service misconfiguration could trigger a data breach that your customers will blame you for, not your vendor.

And yet, third-party risk is often under-resourced and misunderstood. Teams assume that SLAs will protect them, that onboarding due diligence is a one-time task, or that if the vendor is "big enough," it must be safe. But most significant incidents in payments trace back to breakdowns in third-party oversight.

In this chapter, we'll explore:

- How to identify, categorize, and prioritize third-party risks in payments

- Why vendor due diligence must evolve from a checklist to an ongoing discipline.

- How to manage risk across critical dependencies like cloud services, processors, and embedded banking partners

- What regulators expect from third-party governance, and what happens when you fall short?

In the interconnected world of digital finance, your platform is only as strong as the weakest link in your supply chain. Managing third-party risk isn't just about vetting your partners; it's about owning your ecosystem.

Types of Third-Party Risk in Payments

Every third party you rely on, from infrastructure to onboarding, from processing to payouts, introduces risk. But not all vendors are equal, and not all risks look the same. To build a meaningful third-party risk management strategy, payment companies must go beyond surface-level categorizations and understand the specific types of risk third parties can introduce and how those risks show up in real-world scenarios.

At a high level, third-party risks fall into several overlapping categories, each with its impact profile:

Operational Risk

This is the most immediate and visible type of third-party risk: downtime, service failure, or latency introduced by your vendors.

Consider a payment gateway that crashes during Black Friday. Or a cloud provider whose regional data center goes down, taking your transaction API with it. These are not theoretical risks; they are common, high-impact disruptions that affect customer trust, revenue, and brand reputation.

Operational risk also encompasses issues such as missed settlement windows by acquiring banks, payout delays from local partners, or even integration bugs that misroute transactions. In payments, where speed and uptime are non-negotiable, every operational dependency is a risk node.

Compliance and Regulatory Risk

When a vendor touches your customer data, performs KYC, screens for sanctions, or manages funds, any failure on their part can become your liability. Regulators don't differentiate between what's outsourced and what's internal; they care whether you upheld your compliance obligations.

For example, if your AML service fails to flag a sanctioned entity, you're the one facing scrutiny. If your KYC provider lets through a fraudulent business, it's your merchant portfolio that's compromised. And if your banking-as-a-service partner loses its license, your entire offering may be at risk overnight.

This is why regulators now expect companies to audit their vendors, not just contract with them. Due diligence, oversight, and regular performance reviews are no longer optional.

Cybersecurity and Data Risk

Any vendor with access to sensitive data, customer PII, payment credentials, or transaction logs becomes part of your security perimeter.

This includes cloud providers, analytics tools, fraud systems, and even outsourced development teams. If a third party suffers a breach, you're still on the hook for reporting, customer notification, and damage control. Many of the world's most significant data breaches originated not from internal systems, but from compromised vendors.

Additionally, weak vendor controls around access, encryption, and patching can create exploitable backdoors into your infrastructure. And since modern fintech stacks are API-driven, even read-only integrations can become attack vectors if not secured and monitored.

Third-Party Financial Risk

Financial risk from third parties can take several forms:

Processor insolvency: If a small PSP holding your funds goes bankrupt, what recourse do you have?

Settlement failure: If your acquirer delays payouts or mismanages reserve balances, your merchants may lose trust in your platform.

FX volatility: If a cross-border partner executes conversions at unpredictable rates, it can eat into your margins or cause reconciliation headaches.

Some providers may also over-rely on a single funding source or banking relationship. If that upstream entity de-banks them, you may be affected through no fault of your own.

Third Party Strategic and Reputational Risk

Lastly, your vendors reflect your brand. If a third party is exposed for enabling fraudulent transactions, mishandling customer complaints, or violating consumer protection laws, the negative attention lands on you, too.

Consider a payout partner facing public scrutiny for working with fraud merchants. Even if your operation is fully compliant, the association may cause partners, investors, or regulators to question your judgment.

Strategic risk also includes over-dependence on any single vendor. If you rely too heavily on one provider for onboarding, settlement, or infrastructure, you may lose bargaining power, flexibility, or, in the event of failure, continuity.

Risk, Multiplied by Connection

In today's interconnected payments environment, you're not just managing your own risk; you're inheriting the dangers of everyone you depend on. And often, those risks multiply as you scale. What starts as a lightweight integration with a startup KYC vendor can become a critical dependency overnight.

That's why categorizing and understanding these risks early is so important. It's the first step in building a third-party oversight program that protects your platform, not just from what your vendors do wrong, but from what they could do if left unchecked.

Next, we'll explore how to build that oversight, starting with vendor due diligence that goes deeper than the surface.

Vendor Due Diligence: Beyond the Checklist

Every third-party relationship begins with trust, but trust, in risk management, must be earned, verified, and revisited. Too often, due diligence is treated as a one-time formality: a checklist of standard questions, a quick legal review, and a signed contract. But in the world of payments, where third parties can directly influence compliance, stability, and customer experience, this surface-level vetting isn't enough.

Adequate due diligence is not a gate; it's a filter. Its purpose isn't just to approve vendors, but to understand where they fit into your risk exposure, how critical they are to your operations, and how well-prepared they are to uphold your standards over time.

Why Basic Checklists Fall Short

Most vendor onboarding forms include questions about licensing, insurance, uptime guarantees, and privacy policies. These are important, but insufficient. For example:

A vendor may claim to be PCI-compliant but outsource card managing to another firm you've never heard of.

They may pass a SOC 2 audit but fail to implement basic access control on shared environments.

They may promise 99.9% uptime but have no documented incident response plan, or worse, no obligation to notify you when an incident occurs.

These details won't appear on a generic questionnaire. You need to dig deeper.

Designing Meaningful Due Diligence

Strong due diligence goes beyond paperwork. It asks:

➢ What is this vendor's exact role in your ecosystem?

➢ What data do they manage? What systems do they access?

➢ What is the blast radius if they fail, technically, legally, or reputationally?

Depending on the answers, your approach to review should scale accordingly. For critical vendors, such as processors, BaaS partners, or cloud providers, this might mean:

➢ Reviewing audit reports and penetration test results

➢ Asking for detailed architectural diagrams

➢ Assessing key person risk and financial stability

➢ Understanding their subcontractor relationships

➢ Evaluating their compliance with relevant local laws (e.g., GDPR, CCPA, AML directives)

And perhaps most importantly: meeting with their risk, compliance, or technical teams to gauge maturity, transparency, and willingness to collaborate.

Understanding the Limits of Paper Promises

Contracts are essential, but they aren't shields. You can't enforce an SLA if your platform is down and your vendor's team is unresponsive. You can't recover lost trust with merchants or users because a clause said you weren't liable.

This is why due diligence must assess practical capability, not just contractual assurances. For example:

➤ Does the vendor have a working incident response protocol, and do they evaluate it?

➤ Are alerts, support tickets, and compliance requests managed within realistic time limits?

➤ If the vendor is regulated, what's their enforcement history?

➤ How do they manage churn, acquisitions, or business model pivots, and do they inform you?

You're not just evaluating a business; you're evaluating a long-term risk partner.

Making It Ongoing, Not One-Off

Proper due diligence isn't just about onboarding; it's about monitoring. Vendors change. Their financial health, leadership, infrastructure, and security posture evolve. What was acceptable at contract signing may not be safe a year later.

This is why leading organizations implement:

➤ Annual or biannual vendor reviews, tailored to risk level.

➤ Performance scorecards to track SLA adherence and incident history.

➢ Re-certification workflows tied to internal audit cycles.

➢ Exit plans for critical vendors, including backup relationships and transition strategies.

By treating vendor oversight as a lifecycle, not a checklist, you avoid complacency and ensure ongoing alignment with your own risk tolerance and regulatory obligations.

Trust, But Inspect

In an industry where your partners are extensions of your platform, due diligence is not about suspicion; it's about stewardship. It shows that you take your obligations seriously, that you understand your dependencies, and that you won't compromise user trust by leaving risk management to chance.

In the next section, we'll examine what happens after due diligence: how to manage third-party performance and risk in real time, as part of your day-to-day operations.

Ongoing Monitoring and Managing

Selecting the right vendor is just the beginning. In payments, risk doesn't remain static, and neither do your vendors. What begins as a trustworthy, well-documented partnership can shift over time, sometimes subtly, sometimes dramatically. A leadership change, a new product direction, a lapse in controls, or quiet financial distress can all introduce fresh risk into your ecosystem long after the ink on the contract has dried.

That's why the real discipline of third-party risk management lies in what happens after onboarding. Continuous monitoring, encompassing not just technical performance but also operational resilience, compliance posture, and evolving alignment with your business, is what keeps partnerships safe, productive, and scalable.

Monitoring is not about micromanaging your vendors. It's about establishing a line of sight into how they're operating, how they're adapting, and whether they're still meeting the standards you expect, especially when no one is actively watching.

Understanding the Signals of Vendor Risk

The signs that a vendor relationship may be drifting into dangerous territory are rarely dramatic. More often, they begin as small changes: longer response times on support tickets, vague answers during check-ins, increased incidents of delay or error, or a subtle shift in tone during compliance discussions. These are all early indicators that a previously stable vendor may be slipping in quality, capacity, or internal control.

Some platforms only notice these signals once something breaks, such as an outage, a breach, or a fine. But mature organizations design processes to detect them earlier and act before damage spreads.

One example is watching how a vendor manages minor incidents. Do they inform you quickly, or only after prompting? Do they document and share lessons learned, or do they try to minimize exposure? Vendors who are transparent in small things are usually more trustworthy in a crisis.

Integrating Monitoring into Operations

Monitoring isn't just a quarterly review or a shared dashboard. It's embedded in the daily rhythm of collaboration. This includes:

Maintaining open communication channels between your teams and theirs, not just at the executive level, but operationally, where the real work happens.

Tracking SLA adherence over time and looking at patterns, not just if they hit targets, but how consistently, and how they respond when they don't.

Periodically revisit your risk classification for each vendor, especially if they've expanded scope, taken on new responsibilities, or experienced personnel turnover.

Where appropriate, some companies establish joint steering committees or standing calls with critical vendors, particularly when infrastructure or regulatory compliance is involved. These aren't bureaucratic overheads; they're alignment mechanisms, helping ensure that both parties stay informed, accountable, and proactive.

Preparing for the Unpredictable

One of the most overlooked areas of third-party risk is exit planning. What happens if a vendor is acquired, loses its license, or suffers a catastrophic failure? If your entire payout system depends on a single provider with no backup, even a short-term disruption can become an existential threat.

Monitoring should include periodic scenario testing: Could you reroute traffic or switch providers within 72 hours? Do you have access to your data? Can you retrieve customer documentation if your KYC vendor disappears? Planning for these scenarios isn't paranoia, it's preparation.

Likewise, monitoring should evolve with your business. A vendor that was "low risk" when you processed 10,000 transactions per month might become a core dependency when you're processing a million. As your volume, complexity, and regulatory exposure grow, your oversight must scale with it.

Vigilance Builds Trust

You can't watch everything at once. But by staying close to the vendors that matter most, and embedding practical, consistent monitoring into your operations, you shift from a reactive stance to a resilient, proactive posture. You show partners, regulators, and internal stakeholders that you take your ecosystem seriously, and that your trust, like your platform, is earned and maintained over time.

In the next section, we'll turn to what regulators increasingly expect in this area: how to design a formal third-party governance program that aligns with global compliance frameworks and protects your license to operate.

Third-Party Governance and Regulatory Expectations

As the payments industry has matured and grown increasingly dependent on outsourced services, regulators around the world have become far more vocal, and far more specific, about how companies should govern their third-party relationships. It's no longer enough to have a contract in place and a list of vendors on file. Today, regulators expect structured oversight, clear documentation, and evidence that risk management isn't outsourced; only the function is.

Third-party governance is about accountability. It's the system by which you define who your vendors are, how critical they are to your business, how they're vetted and monitored, and what plans are in place if something goes wrong. And increasingly, it's one of the first areas that regulators audit, because weak vendor controls are often the hidden cause behind fraud, outages, data breaches, and compliance violations.

What Regulators Are Looking For

Across jurisdictions, whether you're licensed under PSD2 in the EU, FINTRAC in Canada, MAS in Singapore, or the FCA in the UK, the expectations are converging. Supervisory bodies want to see that payment companies have:

> A centralized inventory of all third-party providers, including subcontractors and affiliates.

➢ Defined risk classification for each vendor based on access, data sensitivity, and criticality.

➢ Due diligence records that go beyond checklists and show real risk assessment.

➢ Evidence of ongoing monitoring, including performance tracking, security review, and SLA compliance.

➢ Incident escalation paths and response plans, especially for critical vendors.

➢ Withdrawal plans, including contingency plans for vendor failure or termination.

For critical outsourcing, such as core banking-as-a-service, settlement operations, or KYC functions, regulators may also expect pre-approval or periodic audits, particularly in high-risk jurisdictions or when sensitive customer data crosses borders.

When Oversight Fails

The consequences of poor vendor governance are no longer theoretical. Regulators have issued fines, revoked licenses, and publicly sanctioned companies that failed to manage their third parties appropriately.

In several high-profile cases, payment platforms faced enforcement not because of what they did, but because a vendor mishandled data, failed to report an incident, or operated beyond their scope. Regulators didn't accept "we didn't know" as a defense. The responsibility always returns to the licensed entity because the risk doesn't go away when you outsource it.

Even large, well-funded fintechs have found themselves under pressure when vendor lapses exposed weaknesses in oversight. A misconfigured cloud server by a third-party development partner. A sanctions-screening provider that missed critical updates. A dispute-resolution partner that failed to meet mandated timelines. Each of these failures, while externally caused, had internal consequences, regulatory, reputational, and financial.

Operationalizing Governance

Governance isn't about building walls of paperwork. It's about embedding apparent, sustainable oversight into your operations. This means:

➤ Assigning vendor owners, someone in the business who is accountable for the performance and risk of each key relationship.

➢ Establishing a third-party risk committee or cross-functional group that reviews vendor onboarding, performance issues, and incident follow-up.

➢ Incorporating vendor review into existing risk reporting and board updates, not treating it as a separate compliance exercise.

➢ Using tooling, from simple dashboards to integrated GRC platforms, to track vendor status, documentation, and renewal timelines in one place.

The goal is to integrate vendor oversight into your institutional muscle, rather than scrambling during audit season.

Governance Is the License to Scale

As regulators raise expectations and third-party ecosystems grow more complex, your ability to govern your vendors becomes inseparable from your ability to succeed. Partners, investors, and compliance reviewers are all asking the same questions: Who do you rely on? How do you manage them? And what happens if they fail?

A strong third-party governance program answers those questions with clarity, structure, and confidence, not just on paper, but in practice.

In the final section of this chapter, we'll bring it all together, exploring how to design a scalable, risk-aligned third-party management strategy that evolves with your platform and supports global expansion.

Building a Scalable Risk Management Strategy

As your payments platform grows into new markets, products, and partnerships, your third-party network will grow with it. What begins as a handful of core vendors can quickly expand into a sprawling ecosystem of integrations, affiliates, sub-processors, and infrastructure providers. Each one brings value. Each one brings risk. And the companies that succeed long-term are the ones that treat this web of connections not as a liability, but as a strategic capability to be managed with intent.

A scalable third-party risk management strategy doesn't mean more bureaucracy. It means building the right frameworks early, lightweight where possible, robust where necessary, so that as your business expands, your ability to manage exposure scales with it.

This begins with clarity. You need to know who your third parties are, what they do, how critical they are to your operations, and where their risks intersect with your obligations. This isn't just about maintaining an inventory; it's about understanding interdependence. For example, a single cloud platform might host both your KYC vendor and your core ledger service. If that platform goes down, your entire user experience is disrupted, even if your systems remain functional.

Risk classification helps you prioritize. A vendor providing marketing analytics may need lighter oversight than a partner managing settlements or issuing prepaid cards. By layering controls according to risk, rather than relying on one-size-fits-all policies, you maintain agile governance without compromising your standards.

Scalability also depends on automation and documentation. Manual review cycles can work for five or ten vendors, but not fifty or more. This is where risk management tooling, whether it's purpose-built software or customized dashboards, plays a key role. These systems help you track due diligence, centralize SLAs and certifications, flag upcoming renewals, and keep audit records in one place. They reduce the overhead of oversight, freeing your teams to focus on judgment rather than paperwork.

But the process is only half the equation. The other half is ownership. For a strategy to scale, responsibility must be distributed. This means giving business units the training and authority to evaluate vendors within their domain, with risk and compliance guiding, not gatekeeping. It also means ensuring that every critical vendor has an internal advocate: someone who can speak to their performance, surface issues early, and lead transitions if needed.

Scalable strategies are also designed for change. They account for the fact that vendors evolve, companies pivot, regulations tighten, and technology moves quickly. A strong third-party risk approach doesn't assume stasis; it builds in checkpoints, escalation paths, and exit options. It gives your company the freedom to grow boldly, without growing recklessly.

Strong Partners, Strong Platform

In the end, managing third-party risk isn't about saying no to partnerships. It's about choosing the right ones, supporting them wisely, and owning the responsibility that comes with every outsourced function. As payments become more embedded, more real-time, and more global, your vendors will touch more of your business than ever before. If you don't manage that exposure with care, no one will do it for you.

A scalable strategy ensures you can keep moving fast, without leaving risk to chance. Because in this ecosystem, your partners aren't just part of your platform; they are part of your promise.

Chapter Summary: Risk You Don't Control

Third-party risk in payments is not a new challenge, but it is one that's become increasingly complex, increasingly visible, and increasingly consequential. As we've explored in this chapter, modern payment platforms don't just collaborate with vendors; they run on them. Cloud infrastructure, KYC providers, banking-as-a-service platforms, API gateways, fraud engines, and payout rails are not support services. They are the operational backbone of digital finance.

And with that dependence comes exposure. When a vendor fails, misbehaves, or falls behind on compliance, the fallout lands at your doorstep. Responsibility may be shared, but accountability is not.

We began by breaking down the types of third-party risk: from obvious concerns like uptime and SLA breaches to less visible but equally dangerous exposures, such as data security failures, regulatory non-compliance, and strategic overreliance. We saw how operational dependencies can become single points of failure, and how reputation can be damaged by proxy when partners act recklessly or unethically.

Then we turned to vendor due diligence, a process too often reduced to checkboxes and file cabinets. But real risk management goes beyond the surface. It asks more complex questions. It examines infrastructure, culture, and incentives. And, most importantly, it continues after the contract is signed. Because vendors change. And so does risk.

We explored the discipline of ongoing monitoring, not as a surveillance tool, but as a relationship strategy. The best companies don't just evaluate vendors; they stay close to them. They track performance trends, escalate early, and prepare for the unexpected. Monitoring, when done well, is a trust-building act and a business continuity safeguard.

We then examined what regulators now demand: structured third-party governance. Across jurisdictions, supervisory bodies expect payment companies to know precisely who they depend on, how they manage those relationships, and how quickly they can respond when something goes wrong. Weak vendor oversight is no longer an internal issue; it's a regulatory liability.

And finally, we looked at how to bring all of this together into a scalable strategy, one that can support growth without sacrificing discipline. From assigning ownership and automating tracking, to designing for change and aligning oversight with risk tiers, we outlined what it takes to build a third-party management program that doesn't buckle under pressure; it gets stronger.

Because in the end, managing third-party risk isn't just about preventing failure. It's about ensuring that the people, platforms, and partners you depend on are worthy of the trust your customers place in you.

In Chapter 9, we'll look ahead to the fast-emerging technologies reshaping the payments landscape, and how companies can prepare for the new kinds of risk they introduce. From AI-driven decision-making and programmable money to quantum security and digital identity, the future is arriving fast. The question is: will your risk framework be ready?

Section 4: The Future of Payments Risk

Chapter 9: Emerging Tech and the Future of Risk

The payments industry has constantly evolved at the edge of innovation, but today, that edge is moving faster than ever. Artificial intelligence, real-time data ecosystems, decentralized finance (DeFi), embedded banking, biometric authentication, and programmable money are no longer theoretical advancements. They are active forces reshaping how money moves, how value is stored, and how trust is managed.

These technologies promise speed, scale, personalization, and automation. They also introduce new attack surfaces, new ethical questions, and new forms of systemic risk. As payment platforms race to integrate the next generation of tools and capabilities, the challenge for risk leaders is no longer just keeping up; it's seeing around corners.

Many of the tools now being adopted, from large language models to blockchain settlement layers, operate in black boxes. Their logic is complex to audit. Their outcomes are hard to predict. Their creators may sit outside traditional financial ecosystems. And yet, they are becoming core infrastructure for onboarding, credit decisioning, identity verification, and transaction routing.

In this chapter, we'll explore:

➢   How AI and machine learning are transforming fraud detection and credit risk, and why they introduce governance and explainability challenges.

➢   The risk landscape of blockchain and DeFi includes smart contract vulnerabilities, asset volatility, and regulatory uncertainty.

➢   The implications of biometric authentication, tokenized identity, and zero-trust infrastructure in a world where digital identity becomes fluid and programmable.

➢   What quantum computing may mean for encryption, and how payment companies can prepare for a disruption that still feels distant but is rushing.

➢   And finally, how to build a forward-looking risk strategy that allows your business to embrace innovation without losing control.

Because the future of payments isn't just about what's possible, it's about what's safe, explainable, and resilient.

And in a world of increasing complexity, the most successful organizations will be those that view risk not as a brake on innovation, but as the design discipline that makes innovation sustainable.

AI and Machine Learning in Payments

Artificial intelligence has become the heartbeat of modern payment infrastructure. From fraud prevention to credit scoring, from transaction routing to customer support, machine learning (ML) systems are now embedded in the decisions that happen billions of times each day, often in milliseconds, often invisibly.

The promise is real. AI enables platforms to analyze more data, faster and with greater nuance, than any human ever could. It detects patterns across devices, behaviors, and networks. It adapts to new fraud tactics in near real time. It scores creditworthiness based on dynamic, alternative data rather than rigid historical rules. It powers chatbots that respond in seconds, and dynamic pricing engines that optimize in real time.

But with this power comes a new category of risk, one that is both technical and ethical, both operational and reputational. Because, unlike traditional systems, AI doesn't just execute logic, it creates it. And that means risk managers must now contend with a form of decision-making that is powerful, opaque, and constantly evolving.

The Risks Lurking Inside the Model

AI systems don't break the way traditional systems do. There's no line of code to debug, no simple on/off switch to flip. Instead, problems arise from data drift, model bias, insufficient training samples, or flawed assumptions embedded deep inside the algorithms.

For example, a fraud detection model might begin over-penalizing transactions from specific geographic regions, not out of malice, but because of skewed historical inputs. A credit risk engine might consistently score thin-file customers lower than they deserve, simply because it hasn't seen enough positive examples. A chatbot might begin suggesting incorrect answers after ingesting corrupted data.

These failures aren't always visible until real harm occurs, a spike in false declines, a regulator asking hard questions, or customers abandoning your platform out of frustration.

And because many AI systems function as "black boxes," even the teams that deploy them often can't fully explain how they reached a decision.

Explainability and Accountability

This is why explainability has become one of the key pillars of responsible AI in payments. It's not enough for an AI to be accurate; it must also be auditable. If a user is declined, can your system justify the decision? If a regulator asks why specific customers are being flagged for enhanced due diligence, can you show the model logic?

Regulators worldwide, including the EU under the AI Act, and U.S. agencies under emerging guidance, are increasingly focused on algorithmic accountability. They expect companies to understand and govern their models, validate them regularly, and demonstrate that AI is being used fairly, securely, and in line with customer rights.

This means building in model risk management frameworks, conducting bias testing, tracking model performance over time, and involving human reviewers in high-stakes or ambiguous decisions.

Operationalizing Safe AI Use

To harness AI responsibly in payments, companies must take deliberate steps:

➤ First, ensure cross-functional oversight. AI should never be the sole domain of a technical team. Risk, compliance, product, and legal functions must collaborate to set model boundaries, define success metrics, and intervene when issues arise.

➢ Second, treat training data as a security asset. Poor-quality or manipulated input data can poison model outputs. Data governance becomes as essential as model architecture.

➢ Third, limit automation in high-risk scenarios. Not every decision should be instant or autonomous. When a significant transaction is flagged as potentially fraudulent, or a user is about to be denied onboarding, it may be better to introduce a manual review path, not just to reduce false positives, but to maintain trust.

➢ Lastly, maintain AI documentation that is readable by humans, not just by engineers. When things go wrong, you need to know what the model was designed to do, how it was trained, when it was last tested, and where the thresholds were set.

The Paradox of Smart Systems

AI brings speed, precision, and insight, but it also brings fragility in new forms. It doesn't make traditional risk management obsolete; it raises the bar. Because while AI can detect risk faster than any analyst, it can also create new types of blind spots that legacy systems never imagined.

In the next section, we'll turn to another frontier technology with both disruptive promise and regulatory uncertainty: blockchain and decentralized finance (DeFi), and what happens when payments no longer require intermediaries at all.

Blockchain, DeFi, and the Risk of Disintermediation

One of the most profound shifts in the payments industry isn't just technological, it's philosophical. Traditional finance is built on intermediaries: banks, processors, clearinghouses, and regulators that oversee and secure the movement of money. But blockchain and decentralized finance (DeFi) challenge that very premise. In their ideal form, they remove the need for centralized trust altogether.

On a public blockchain, value moves directly between users. Smart contracts automate settlement. Liquidity pools replace traditional banks. Anyone with an internet connection and a wallet can send, receive, lend, or trade assets, often without identity verification, regulatory oversight, or the intervention of a trusted third party.

The promise is compelling: faster settlement, lower fees, open access. But for payment companies, especially those operating in regulated environments, DeFi doesn't eliminate risk. It relocates it. And in many cases, it introduces entirely new categories of exposure that don't exist in traditional systems.

The Allure and the Ambiguity

To understand the risk of disintermediation, one must first understand its appeal. Blockchain-based payment systems offer real-time settlement across borders, programmable money that can trigger automatically based on contract logic, and the ability to build financial services that are composable, transparent, and censorship-resistant.

But they also come with a few guardrails. If a smart contract has a bug, the funds may be lost forever. If a protocol is exploited, there is often no recourse. If a token issuer vanishes, the asset may become worthless, instantly.

And for platforms integrating blockchain rails or enabling crypto-based transactions, the risks become your risks, even if the infrastructure is decentralized.

Smart Contracts, Real-World Consequences

One of the most unique elements of DeFi is the smart contract: self-executing code that runs on a blockchain, often managing the logic for payments, lending, or asset exchanges. These contracts are powerful, but also brittle. Once deployed, they are immutable. If the logic is flawed, or if an attacker discovers a loophole, millions of dollars can be drained in minutes, as has happened countless times on platforms like Ethereum.

Brilliant contract exploits are not theoretical edge cases. They are common, lucrative, and challenging to prevent. For payment companies integrating with or building on these systems, code becomes law, and risk managers must learn to speak its language.

AML, KYC, and the Compliance Vacuum

DeFi's pseudonymous nature poses significant challenges for compliance. Users often interact with platforms via wallet addresses, not verified identities. This makes traditional Know Your Customer (KYC) protocols difficult to apply and Anti-Money Laundering (AML) obligations hard to enforce.

As regulators begin to scrutinize these systems more closely, companies that offer access to decentralized protocols, even indirectly, may be held responsible for ensuring compliance, monitoring flows, and reporting suspicious activity. In the eyes of regulators, "permissionless" doesn't mean "responsibility-free."

This is already unfolding. FATF guidance now includes "Virtual Asset Service Providers" (VASPs) in its framework, and jurisdictions like the EU and U.S. are considering how to extend existing rules to cover DeFi platforms and facilitators. For companies operating in hybrid models, blending traditional payments with blockchain rails, clarity is still evolving, but the risk is real.

Custody, Volatility, and Irreversibility

Even beyond compliance, DeFi and blockchain introduce operational risks:

➢ Custody: Holding or transmitting digital assets requires airtight security. Hot wallets, multi-signature controls, and secure key management are no longer optional; they are survival mechanisms.

➢ Volatility: Crypto asset values can swing dramatically, turning a $100 settlement into $70 in minutes. Without dynamic hedging, FX protection, or stablecoin options, platforms face exposure.

➢ Finality: Blockchain transactions are irreversible. If a customer sends funds to the wrong address, there's no support line to call. For platforms that aim to provide consumer protection, this creates a disconnect between user expectations and technical reality.

The Risk of the Middleman Being You

Ironically, as platforms integrate DeFi capabilities to "remove intermediaries," they may become the de facto intermediary in the eyes of both users and regulators. They offer the front end, facilitate access, provide user support, and manage the fallout when things go wrong.

This means that even if you don't control the protocol, you must maintain your risk posture around it.

In the next section, we'll explore another fast-evolving domain that sits at the intersection of security and identity: biometrics, digital credentials, and the future of trust in payments.

Biometrics, Digital Identity, and the Risks of Hyper-Personalization

As digital payments become more seamless, identity is becoming more central and more personal. Face scans, fingerprints, voice recognition, and behavioral biometrics are replacing passwords and PINs. At the same time, a new wave of identity infrastructure is emerging digital IDs, verifiable credentials, and decentralized identity wallets that promise users complete control over their data and authentication.

In theory, this next evolution of digital identity solves major problems. It improves user experience, reduces fraud, and enables more secure onboarding. But in practice, it introduces a new and complex frontier of risk, one where the boundary between person and platform is increasingly blurred.

Biometric and identity data aren't just sensitive, they're irreplaceable. You can change a password. You can't change your iris.

The Promise: Frictionless and Fraud-Resistant

Biometric authentication has surged in popularity because it offers something both users and platforms crave security without friction. A fingerprint unlocks a wallet app in seconds. A face scan authorizes a transaction faster than typing a code. Even passive indicators like keystroke cadence or mouse movement can validate user presence.

Meanwhile, digital identity wallets, particularly those built on decentralized or government-verified credentials, give users control over what they share and with whom. For cross-border payments, where identity verification is fragmented and inconsistent, these tools could offer a unified, portable solution.

For platforms, this means fewer drop-offs during onboarding, faster fraud detection, and a more seamless KYC experience.

But the same technologies that create smoother flows also create deeper dependencies and new forms of vulnerability.

When Identity Becomes the Attack Surface

Biometric data, once compromised, becomes a permanent threat vector. A stolen fingerprint or deepfaked face can be reused across platforms, especially those that don't cross-reference with behavioral signals or secondary verification layers.

Attackers have already begun exploiting these systems. From spoofed voice commands to 3D facial models, the tools to mimic a person's identity are rapidly advancing. And because biometrics are often used as sole authentication, a successful compromise gives attackers near-total access.

Likewise, decentralized digital ID systems, while empowering users, may become difficult for platforms to validate or revoke. If a user presents a verifiable credential from a compromised issuer, who bears the liability? If a credential is tied to a blockchain, how is fraud redressed when the data is immutable?

These are not theoretical concerns. They are design flaws waiting to become incidents, unless mitigated through layered verification, risk scoring, and fallback recovery paths.

Regulatory and Ethical Dimensions

The regulatory scrutiny around biometric and identity systems is growing fast. Laws like the EU's GDPR, California's CCPA, and India's DPDP Act place strict boundaries on how identity and biometric data can be collected, stored, and processed.

Payment platforms that fail to obtain proper consent, offer opt-out mechanisms, or secure this data at rest and in motion risk severe fines and reputational damage. And beyond regulation, there are ethical questions: What happens when identity scoring systems reinforce bias? What happens when users are denied access due to outdated or misread biometrics?

As systems become more personal, they also become more political. Risk leaders must not only secure these technologies but also ensure they are fair, inclusive, and explainable.

Operationalizing Trust in Identity

To manage the risks of hyper-personalized authentication and identity:

➢ Treat biometric data as high-risk PII, with enhanced encryption, storage isolation, and breach protocols.

➢ Avoid single-point dependency, use biometrics as part of multi-factor authentication, not in place of it.

➢ Monitor for behavioral anomalies, not just static matches, by combining passive data (such as typing speed, device ID, and usage patterns) with active factors.

➢ Ensure users have recovery options in case biometrics fail or devices are lost, particularly for financial access.

Most importantly, be transparent. Inform users about the verification process for their identity, the data stored, and their rights to revoke or manage access.

Identity Is Infrastructure, and Vulnerability

In the future of payments, identity is the key to everything: onboarding, authentication, transaction approval, and even dispute resolution. But the more personalized the system becomes, the more damage it can do when it breaks.

Payments companies that embrace identity innovation without embedding risk safeguards will find themselves facing not just technical threats, but regulatory, reputational, and ethical ones.

In the next section, we'll peer even further into the horizon: quantum computing and the potential collapse of today's cryptographic standards, and what payments leaders must start preparing for now.

Quantum Risk and the Future of Encryption

If there is one technological shift capable of disrupting the very foundations of modern payments, it is quantum computing. Still in its early stages, this emerging field promises to solve complex problems millions of times faster than classical computers. But with that leap comes a threat of equal magnitude: the potential to break the cryptographic algorithms that secure global financial infrastructure.

Today's payment systems, from APIs and transaction rails to identity verification and blockchain, rely heavily on cryptography. Protocols like RSA, ECC (Elliptic Curve Cryptography), and AES underlie the encryption standards used to protect sensitive data in transit, verify digital signatures, and authorize transactions. These methods are considered mathematically secure against current forms of attack.

Quantum computers could change that—and not decades from now, potentially within the next 10 to 15 years.

What Makes Quantum So Dangerous (and Inevitable)

Classical computers solve problems step by step. Quantum computers, through properties like superposition and entanglement, can evaluate multiple outcomes simultaneously. This makes them uniquely powerful at factoring large numbers and solving specific algorithms. These two abilities directly threaten the security of RSA and ECC, the cryptographic workhorses of the payments industry.

A sufficiently advanced quantum computer could, in theory, decrypt communications, forge digital signatures, and reverse encryption keys once thought unbreakable. This would effectively render current cryptographic standards obsolete and open the door to mass data compromise, transaction forgery, and trust collapse across digital payment networks.

Even more concerning is the notion of "store now, decrypt later" attacks. Adversaries may already be capturing and storing encrypted data, with the intent of decrypting it once quantum capabilities mature.

The Emerging Discipline of Post-Quantum Cryptography

The race to counter this risk is already underway. Governments, academia, and industry groups are working on post-quantum cryptographic (PQC) algorithms designed to withstand quantum attacks. In 2022, the U.S. National Institute of Standards and Technology (NIST) announced its first round of selected PQC algorithms, beginning the path toward standardization.

But adoption will take time. These algorithms are larger, slower, and not yet universally supported. Migrating payment systems, many of which are deeply integrated with legacy infrastructure, will require significant planning, testing, and coordination.

For now, quantum risk remains a strategic, long-horizon threat. But the decisions made today, especially around cryptographic agility and data lifecycle management, will determine whether payment companies can respond quickly when the time comes.

What Payments Companies Can Do Today

Inventory Your Cryptographic Dependencies

Start by understanding where and how cryptography is used in your stack. What algorithms protect your APIs, your data at rest, your digital signatures, and your blockchain keys? Are those systems flexible enough to support new cryptographic schemes?

Design for Cryptographic Agility

Future-ready systems must be able to swap out cryptographic algorithms without a complete overhaul. This means modular design, external key management, and avoiding hardcoded protocols.

Limit Long-Term Exposure

If data must be encrypted and stored for years, especially sensitive financial or identity data, consider encrypting it with hybrid models or preparing to re-encrypt as PQC standards mature.

Follow PQC Standardization Efforts

Monitor initiatives from NIST, ISO, and industry consortia. Engage vendors and partners about their plans for PQC adoption, especially if they manage critical components like payment rails or cloud encryption.

Plan for Transition, Not Panic

The move to PQC won't happen overnight. But early investment in awareness, readiness, and optionality will reduce your exposure and give your platform a competitive edge when regulators and partners start asking for quantum resilience.

Quantum: A Future Threat

Quantum computing may still be a few breakthroughs away from impacting day-to-day payments. But in risk management, horizon threats are the ones most likely to catch you unprepared. And when the foundation of digital trust, cryptography itself, is at stake, preparation becomes an existential imperative.

In the final section of this chapter, we'll look at how all these forces —AI, DeFi, biometrics, and quantum —point to one conclusion: risk is no longer a static function. To keep up, organizations must build future-facing risk programs that are agile, experimental, and embedded into innovation from the start.

Designing a Future-Ready Risk Function

The payments industry is entering an era where innovation is not linear; it's exponential. Technologies like AI, blockchain, biometrics, and quantum computing are redefining not only what's possible but also how risk manifests, evolves, and escapes traditional controls. In this environment, risk management cannot remain a backward-looking compliance checklist. It must become a forward-facing, adaptive discipline, deeply embedded in product development, platform architecture, and strategic decision-making.

A future-ready risk function doesn't just respond to threats. It anticipates them. It evolves alongside the business. It's built with enough structure to ensure accountability and enough flexibility to navigate uncertainty.

Risk as a Strategic Enabler

In the past, risk was often seen as a drag on innovation, the group that slowed things down, blocked launches, or added red tape. But in the new era of payments, risk is becoming a core driver of competitive advantage. Companies that understand, control, and communicate their risk posture earn faster approvals from regulators, stronger partnerships with banks, and deeper trust from customers.

In this sense, risk isn't about saying "no", it's about saying "yes, safely." Yes, to real-time settlements, yes to embedded finance, yes to global expansion, but with the guardrails that prevent catastrophic failure.

Key Characteristics of Future-Ready Risk Functions

Technically Fluent: Risk leaders must understand how machine learning models are trained, how smart contracts execute, and how APIs expose attack surfaces. Technical literacy is no longer optional.

Cross-Functional by Design: Future risk teams don't work in silos. They collaborate daily with engineering, product, security, legal, and customer experience teams. They help shape the architecture, not just review it.

Data-Driven and Real-Time: Static dashboards are being replaced by streaming insights, anomaly detection engines, and real-time threat feeds. Risk teams must operate at the same velocity as the platforms they protect.

Experiment-Ready: New threats often emerge in gray areas, unintended outcomes of new features or tools. A future-ready risk function embraces testing, runs simulations, and learns quickly from near misses.

Scenario-Aware: Preparedness comes not from guessing the future, but from modeling how systems fail. Horizon scanning, red-teaming, and tabletop exercises are core tools, not rare events.

Governance-Aware, But Not Governance-Bound: Compliance remains essential, but it's the floor, not the ceiling. Risk functions must help interpret ambiguous regulations, guide ethical decision-making, and respond to novel challenges regulators haven't yet codified.

Risk as a Source of Confidence

In the most resilient payment organizations, risk doesn't slow down growth; it makes it sustainable. It doesn't eliminate uncertainty; it helps teams navigate it. And it doesn't sit in a silo; it runs alongside product, strategy, and engineering like a co-pilot.

Designing a future-ready risk function means thinking in systems, planning for failure, and building trust, not just in users, but in the infrastructure of your organization. The risks ahead are complex. The tools are evolving. The threats are faster.

But so is the opportunity, for those who are prepared.

Chapter Summary: Facing Forward

The future of payments is already unfolding. Tools once considered experimental, such as artificial intelligence, decentralized finance, digital identity systems, and quantum-aware protocols, are becoming the new foundation on which financial systems are being built. With that evolution comes a new landscape of risk: dynamic, fast-moving, and often operating beyond the reach of traditional controls.

In this chapter, we explored what it means to navigate that landscape with both curiosity and caution.

We began with AI and machine learning, which are transforming fraud prevention, credit risk, and operations. Their power is undeniable, but so are their pitfalls. Opaque logic, algorithmic bias, and unmonitored automation introduce risks that must be governed through explainability, accountability, and cross-functional oversight.

We then examined blockchain and DeFi, which promise disintermediation and global accessibility, yet expose platforms to brilliant contract exploits, compliance gray zones, and asset volatility. As platforms adopt these technologies, they must be cautious not to inherit their chaos without implementing their controls.

Biometrics and digital identity represent the next evolution in trust, making authentication faster and more secure. However, when identity becomes the attack surface, platforms must safeguard the data that users can't replace, including faces, fingerprints, and digital reputations. The balance between personalization and protection is more delicate than ever.

We looked ahead to quantum computing, a threat not yet fully realized, but one capable of undermining the cryptographic infrastructure that underpins the entire industry. Preparing for it now, through cryptographic agility and horizon planning, is the difference between resilience and irrelevance.

And finally, we brought these ideas together through the lens of a future-ready risk function, one that isn't tethered to yesterday's frameworks, but engineered to adapt, anticipate, and enable innovation safely. Risk is no longer a reactive tool; it's a strategic capability that strengthens products, builds trust, and ensures longevity.

If there's one theme that defines this chapter, and indeed the future of risk management in payments, it's this:

What's coming next isn't just faster or wiser. It's different. And we must be ready to meet it not with fear, but with fluency.

In the final chapter, we'll bring the book to a close by looking at how all these ideas, from operational controls to emerging threats, come together to form a modern, resilient, and opportunity-ready risk strategy for the payments industry.

Chapter 10: Case Studies in Risk

Risk management theory is only as valuable as its real-world application. In payments, some of the most profound lessons come not from frameworks or policies, but from what happens when things go wrong, or right.

This chapter brings the abstract to life. Through real-world case studies, we'll examine how payment companies, fintech platforms, and even traditional institutions have navigated, and sometimes mishandled, risk in practice. These stories offer more than just cautionary tales. They reveal:

➢ What misaligned incentives and fast growth can outpace controls

➢ What happens when compliance is deprioritized in favor of product velocity.

➢ How well-executed risk frameworks can contain damage and rebuild trust.

➢ The signals that were missed, and how they could have been caught.

Each case is reconstructed to highlight key decisions, risk signals, failures of execution, and moments of clarity. We won't name every company, but the patterns are drawn from publicly documented events, regulatory actions, and direct industry experience.

As you read, consider how these scenarios apply to your organization:

> Would you have caught the early signs?

> Would your teams have known how to respond?

> Would your systems have scaled with the threat?

Let's begin with a case that shook the fintech world: a fraud ring that exploited a platform's onboarding model and caused tens of millions in chargebacks.

Case Study 1: The Onboarding Loophole

A fast-growing fintech platform, celebrated for its sleek interface and lightning-fast account activation, became the target of an aggressive synthetic fraud ring, one that would ultimately exploit its onboarding model and cost the company over $30 million in chargebacks and fines.

The platform offered early wage access and small cash advances to newly onboarded users, with minimal friction. To maximize growth, they had optimized their KYC process around speed. Users only needed to upload a selfie, provide a government-issued ID, and connect a bank account. Document verification was automated and processed in under 60 seconds. The company's marketing team boasted that new users could access funds in "under two minutes."

Initially, this velocity drove massive user adoption and investor enthusiasm. Monthly active accounts tripled in under a year. But in the background, a different set of users was onboarding, synthetic identities.

These weren't stolen identities. They were manufactured, pieced together from real Social Security numbers, AI-generated profile photos, and fabricated addresses. The fraudsters used VPNs to mask IP addresses, employed bots to automate registration, and leveraged drop shipping services to receive physical mail.

Because the company's risk team had limited influence over product timelines, the onboarding engine lacked deeper behavioral analysis. No biometric liveness checks were in place. There were no velocity controls on device fingerprinting or ID reuse. And, critically, the system wasn't designed to flag clusters of new users sharing subtle anomalies, such as similar routing numbers, device types, or email naming patterns.

The synthetic accounts passed onboarding and requested advances. Initially, small amounts, such as $100 and $200, were used; then larger amounts were used once the system had "trusted" them. Within three weeks, they had collectively withdrawn over $9 million. By the time the fraud team escalated concerns, the problem was systemic. Internal estimates suggested more than 15,000 synthetic accounts were active.

When banks began rejecting repayments and users stopped responding to emails, the company discovered the full scope of the breach. But recovery options were limited. The funds were gone. The fraudsters had used instant disbursement features, often cashing out via prepaid cards or crypto exchanges within hours.

The damage wasn't limited to financial loss. Several banks and payment processors severed ties, citing concerns about due diligence. A regulatory audit revealed that while the company had a documented KYC policy, it was not consistently enforced. The result was a multi-agency investigation and a $12 million fine for AML and data oversight failures.

What We Learned from Case Study 1: The KYC That Wasn't Enough

Context

The platform was growing fast. It offered instant account creation and payouts for freelancers, creators, and gig workers. The onboarding flow had been optimized to reduce friction, a short form, basic ID upload, and automatic verification against a third-party database. Time to activation: under five minutes.

Leadership celebrated the growth, marked by tens of thousands of new accounts, high transaction volumes, and an expanding regional reach. But risk and compliance teams had raised quiet concerns. The identity verification process was too light. High-risk countries were being allowed without escalation. Velocity thresholds were generous, sometimes non-existent.

Still, the fraud numbers looked stable until they weren't.

Signals Missed

The platform was being targeted, not by individuals, but by organized fraud rings using synthetic identities.

Hundreds of accounts shared overlapping personal details: slightly modified names, shared phone numbers, or addresses that didn't match local postal records.

Device fingerprints repeated, sometimes tied to dozens of accounts.

Several newly onboarded users immediately attempted high-value transfers or engaged in multi-party routing patterns.

These patterns were detectable, but no one was looking across the systems. The onboarding team only saw what was needed to activate an account. The fraud team was focused on disputes, not origin points. And the compliance team had no real-time access to the data until weeks later.

Each team had a puzzle piece. No one had the picture.

Consequences

Within two weeks, the platform had unknowingly activated more than 1,200 fraudulent accounts. Many had successfully routed money through the system, in some cases laundering funds through short-term payment loops involving shell accounts and external crypto wallets.

The financial loss reached seven figures. But the reputational damage was worse. A major bank partner demanded an audit. The third-party KYC vendor was pulled into a legal review. Regulators in two countries opened inquiries. Internal morale cratered as teams worked around the clock to identify and close synthetic networks, some of which had now embedded themselves deeper into the system.

Worse still, the fraud hadn't stopped. Fraudsters had learned the platform's risk posture and were scaling up attacks.

What Should Have Been in Place

Tiered onboarding workflows that applied higher scrutiny for high-risk geographies or document anomalies.

Behavioral analytics at onboarding, including device fingerprinting, IP intelligence, and velocity-based flagging.

A cross-functional fraud review committee for suspicious onboarding patterns, involving product, compliance, and fraud teams, meets weekly.

Continuous monitoring in the first day's post-activation, when synthetic identities often make their moves.

The issue wasn't that the system missed a signal. The system was never designed to see the signal in the first place.

Takeaway

Fast onboarding without layered identity controls isn't scalable; it's exposure. And synthetic fraud doesn't knock. It walks right in.

Case Study 2: The High-Risk Merchant

A mid-sized payment service provider (PSP), once considered a rising star in the embedded finance space, found itself under investigation by major card networks and facing the threat of de-platforming. The trigger wasn't a single catastrophic incident; it was a slow-building pattern of chargebacks, brand damage, and regulatory concern tied to a rapidly growing portfolio of high-risk merchants.

At first, the PSP's success seemed unstoppable. By offering fast onboarding, developer-friendly APIs, and aggressive revenue-sharing models, and attracted a wave of e-commerce and digital services merchants that traditional acquirers had underserved. Monthly transaction volume doubled in six months. New merchant activations were celebrated as a key growth metric.

But buried within this success were risk signals the company wasn't yet mature enough to interpret.

Many of the new merchants fell into what the networks classify as "high-risk" categories: dietary supplements, drop-shipped electronics, adult content, and trial-based subscription services. These businesses often experience high refund rates, elevated chargebacks, and regulatory complaints, particularly when marketing is aggressive or fulfillment is unreliable.

The PSP's initial risk controls were designed for volume, not nuance. Onboarding processes relied on basic KYB checks, name, tax ID, domain verification, and automated fraud scoring. Little attention was paid to marketing practices, fulfillment models, or historical dispute patterns. And because revenue was tied directly to merchant volume, there was internal resistance to slowing down.

By the time chargeback rates started climbing above the 1% Visa and Mastercard thresholds, the company found itself on the radar of the card networks. Several merchants were placed into monitoring programs like Visa's VDMP and Mastercard's MATCH list. The PSP received formal warnings, urging tighter oversight, or risk being labeled a high-risk aggregator themselves.

To make matters worse, multiple consumer protection agencies had received complaints about deceptive subscription billing practices among some of the merchants. In some cases, users believed they were signing up for a one-time product, only to be billed monthly without clear opt-outs. The reputational fallout started to mount.

The PSP scrambled to respond. It hired external
consultants, paused onboarding in specific verticals, and
built a new risk scoring model. But damage was already
done. Key banking partners grew uneasy, and one
processing relationship was suspended, cutting off a third
of their transaction capacity overnight.

Internally, the leadership team acknowledged the
issue: they had scaled faster than their risk governance
could manage. The PSP had accepted too many merchants
without understanding their business models, and once
volume was flowing, it became challenging to reverse.

Eventually, the company implemented a high-risk
review committee, segmented merchant risk tiers, and
began reviewing marketing flows before activation. But
not before losing several top-performing merchants, and
spending millions in fines, consultant fees, and reserve
requirements to regain trust.

What We Learned from Case Study 2: The Merchant That Grew Too Fast

Context

The platform was a mid-sized payment facilitator
serving e-commerce merchants across the U.S. and
Canada. It had recently relaxed onboarding requirements
to accelerate growth in key verticals, particularly digital

subscriptions and health supplements. One merchant stood out for its meteoric rise: within two weeks of onboarding, they had gone from processing a few hundred dollars a day to nearly $100,000.

Operations took notice, but with the volume came revenue, and the numbers looked good. The platform celebrated the win and moved on.

Signals Missed

The warning signs were there, but no one owned them.

Transaction velocity had jumped tenfold in less than a week.

The merchant's refund rate was climbing, hitting 15% by week three.

Their website content had changed, subtly at first, shifting from general wellness supplements to unverified weight-loss pills marketed with exaggerated claims.

A backend flag indicated that several billing descriptors had been changed, likely to avoid customer recognition on bank statements.

Individually, these issues might have seemed like operational noise. But together, they painted a clear picture: the merchant was pivoting into a high-risk, high-dispute business model, without notifying the platform.

No one flagged it.

Why? Because velocity monitoring, content reviews, and refund analytics lived in different tools, owned by other teams. There was no unified signal, no cross-functional review cadence, and no single point of contact responsible for escalating merchant behavior post-onboarding.

Consequences

By the end of the month, the merchant had processed over $2 million.

Then the chargebacks hit.

Within six weeks, the merchant's chargeback rate exceeded 3%. They were placed into the card network's high-risk monitoring program. The platform, now facing scrutiny, had to claw back funds, issue mass refunds, and justify its onboarding and monitoring process to its acquiring bank.

Reputation took a hit. Risk controls were deemed insufficient. Worse, several other merchants in the same vertical had quietly adopted similar tactics, emboldened by the lack of enforcement.

It wasn't just one bad merchant. It was the start of a pattern.

What Should Have Been in Place

A tiered risk review system for fast-scaling merchants, triggering manual checks once velocity exceeds a predefined threshold.

Ongoing content monitoring to detect changes in product categories and marketing claims.

Refund velocity alerts are integrated into the risk dashboard, not siloed in support tools.

A clear ownership model for merchant lifecycle risk, with defined escalation paths and documentation workflows.

None of this required new technology; only better coordination, better communication, and shared accountability were needed.

Takeaway

Unchecked growth is a risk vector. Merchant success without monitoring is not a win; it's a vulnerability waiting to be exploited.

Case Study 3: The Fraud Pattern

At first, the uptick in chargebacks seemed isolated, a few unusual transactions from a cluster of digital wallet users. Then it spread. Within weeks, a top-tier fintech discovered that its rules-based fraud engine was no longer keeping up with the pace or complexity of attacks. The cost? Over $20 million in losses and a months-long rebuild of their risk infrastructure.

The company, known for its clean UI and customer-first ethos, had built a reputation on offering near-instant transactions and low-friction signup. Its fraud system had been assembled rapidly during the early growth phase and was a patchwork of static rules, simple logic such as flagging unusually high-value transactions, mismatched billing data, or failed login attempts.

The system worked until it didn't.

The fraud pattern was subtle. Attackers began testing cards with small transactions spaced just far enough apart to avoid triggering rate limits. Once validated, they used the accounts to launder funds through peer transfers and prepaid card withdrawals. The fraud wasn't concentrated. It was distributed, slow-burning, and designed to fly below the radar of each rule.

Meanwhile, the fraud engine grew bloated. Dozens of reactive rules had been layered over time in response to past incidents. These rules often contradict each other, leading to false positives and cumbersome escalations. Analysts were overwhelmed by low-value alerts, while the actual fraud slipped through untouched.

A tipping point came when a major card issuer flagged a coordinated ring using the fintech's platform to cycle stolen card data through hundreds of accounts. The chargebacks rolled in days later, too late for recovery.

In the postmortem, several themes emerged:

➢ The fraud models had not been retrained in over a year.

➢ There was no internal fraud science team; instead, operations manually adjusted thresholds.

➢ There were no tools to evaluate new rules in a sandbox or simulate the effect of changes.

➢ And worst of all, fraudsters had begun sharing rule gaps online in real-time.

The executive team was stunned. How could this have gone undetected?

The answer was simple: their tools hadn't kept pace with their threat surface. While user growth had tripled, fraud infrastructure had remained flat. There were no machine learning models, no adaptive scoring, and no behavioral fingerprinting. The fraud team was fighting a drone war with swords.

Eventually, the company brought in data scientists, rebuilt its monitoring stack, and introduced a dynamic risk engine that scored users across dozens of signals. But the reputational hit was real. Banks imposed stricter reserves. Auditors demanded tighter controls. And the product roadmap had to be delayed while risk took priority.

What We Learned from Case Study 3: When the Vendor Failed First

Context

The platform had recently expanded into a new region, enabling cross-border payouts through a local banking API partner. The integration had been fast, just six weeks from handshake to production, and leadership was eager to announce "instant international payouts" as a differentiator in their marketing.

The partner bank provided the required KYC, FX handling, and disbursement rails. From the platform's perspective, the risk had been "outsourced." After all, the vendor was licensed and had passed an initial diligence checklist. Integration testing had been light, but the system worked until it didn't.

Signals Missed

For weeks, the platform had seen intermittent disbursement failures in the new region. Payouts were being delayed or rejected, but users weren't always notified. Support teams flagged the issue repeatedly, but engineering treated it as a service degradation, not a risk event.

Then came the regulatory notice. The partner bank was being investigated for KYC violations and funds mismanagement. Some user funds had been frozen. Others were missing.

Internally, red flags had been accumulating:

The vendor had missed two quarterly SLA reports.

Their IP logs showed inconsistent access patterns, with admin changes during off-hours.

Support cases from high-volume users had spiked, indicating growing trust issues, but the complaints weren't linked back to the vendor.

No one had done a vendor security audit or financial health check since the contract was signed.

The vendor had begun to fail quietly, and the platform didn't know until the damage was public.

Consequences

The platform was suddenly in the crosshairs. Users who lost funds didn't blame the vendor; they blamed the product they used. Regulatory authorities reached out for explanations and remediation plans. The platform had to halt payouts in the affected region, triggering a wave of churn among international creators and freelancers who relied on timely earnings.

Legal costs mounted. Internal trust broke down between the product, legal, and finance teams. Business development paused expansion talks. What started as a vendor issue became an enterprise risk event, all because no one was watching the dependency closely enough.

What Should Have Been in Place

A formal third-party risk program, with scheduled audits, compliance reviews, and system health checks.

Ongoing vendor performance monitoring, not just uptime, but error codes, settlement delays, and support escalations tied to specific partners.

A vendor risk tiering model, flagging when partners touch funds, user identity, or regulated data, and assigning higher scrutiny accordingly.

Internal contingency planning: what to do if the partner goes offline, loses a license, or is compromised.

The platform had focused entirely on its controls, without considering that a trusted partner could become the weakest link.

Takeaway

You can outsource services, but not accountability. Vendor failures don't stay external for long.

Case Study 4: The Compliance Breach

The product launch was supposed to be a milestone, a seamless, one-click international transfer feature that would differentiate the company from its competitors. Instead, it became the beginning of a regulatory unraveling that cost millions in legal fees, eroded partner trust, and nearly forced the company to exit a key market.

The fintech in question operated a cross-border payments platform, primarily targeting freelancers and remote workers needing to move funds between regions. Its initial infrastructure was lean but well-structured: local banking partners, clear KYC flows, and conservative transaction limits during onboarding. But the company's leadership was under pressure, and investors wanted faster expansion into emerging markets.

To reduce friction, product teams were asked to "optimize the user journey" in high-potential countries where documentation verification was inconsistent and infrastructure was weak. What followed was a quiet series of product changes: lower onboarding thresholds, simplified ID upload requirements, and region-based overrides that allowed users in less-regulated jurisdictions to begin transacting before full verification was completed.

No one considered it a compliance breach at the time. The changes were incremental, and the internal assumption was that the risk team could "backfill" verifications as needed. Early metrics looked great, conversion surged, and activation rates doubled.

But under the surface, the platform was onboarding thousands of users without meeting baseline AML/KYC obligations, particularly in high-risk corridors. Eventually, a journalist covering fraud in remittance platforms uncovered a network of fake accounts operating on the fintech's infrastructure. The story broke nationally.

Shortly after, regulators launched a formal investigation. They found that the platform had no consistent enforcement of its verification rules across markets and that product-driven overrides had created systemic exposure. Several financial partners froze access, citing breach of contract. The company's operating license in one district was suspended pending review.

What began as a product shortcut to improve UX had become a full-blown compliance crisis.

What We Learned from Case Study 4: The Inquiry That Turned Into an Emergency

Context

The platform had grown rapidly in three markets over 18 months, with users in both consumer and business segments. It operated as a hybrid, part payment facilitator, part digital wallet, and supported a growing mix of domestic and cross-border transfers.

The company had a small compliance team, comprising a few people who worked across multiple jurisdictions, often pulled into late-stage product reviews or customer escalations. There was no formal licensing team, no policy management platform, and no unified regulatory roadmap. Instead, compliance was often "plugged in as needed."

It worked, until it didn't.

Signals Missed

The initial email seemed routine: a regional regulator requesting information about the platform's data handling practices, user onboarding controls, and transaction monitoring obligations under local law. But no one knew who owned the response. Legal thought compliance was managing it. Compliance thought legal had escalated it to the board. Meanwhile, the regulator received no reply for 21 days.

That's when the tone shifted. A formal investigation was opened.

The platform scrambled to respond, and in the process uncovered deeper issues:

Several products had been launched without jurisdictional reviews, relying on assumptions about cross-border thresholds and exemptions.

Terms of service were inconsistent across regions, with outdated language referencing obsolete risk controls.

The platform had never registered for a required money service business license in one of its fastest-growing markets.

Internal records of AML reviews, sanctions screenings, and merchant onboarding approvals were fragmented or missing entirely.

The problem wasn't evil intent; it was unclear ownership, poor documentation, and a reactive culture that treated compliance as a cost, not a competency.

Consequences

The regulator issued a temporary stop order for new user onboarding in the affected country. Investors demanded a board-level compliance review. A bank partner froze settlement of funds until remediation plans were provided. And internally, trust in leadership eroded as departments blamed one another for the breakdown.

The platform had to spend millions to conduct a third-party compliance audit, rebuild its licensing program, and renegotiate partner terms. Market expansion paused. Hiring slowed. And the brand, once praised for its innovation, became known in the industry for regulatory sloppiness.

This wasn't a single failure. It was the natural result of scaling without integrating compliance into the core of the business.

What Should Have Been in Place

A centralized regulatory register tracking license requirements, application status, and geographic risk exposure.

A dedicated regulatory operations function to coordinate responses, manage filings, and ensure documentation was complete and current.

A clear escalation and response protocol for inquiries, including ownership, timeline, and board-level visibility.

Proactive compliance reviews are embedded in product development, not rushed in afterward.

When compliance is treated as an afterthought, risk doesn't disappear; it accumulates quietly until the regulator finds it first.

Takeaway

Regulatory failure rarely begins with malice; it begins with neglect. And regulators don't just expect answers; they expect ownership.

Case Study 5: The Platform Advantage

While most stories of risk in payments revolve around failures and recovery, this one stands out for a different reason: a platform that built risk into its culture from day one and used it as a competitive edge.

This digital payments company entered a saturated market. Its competitors offered faster onboarding, more features, and aggressive pricing. From a purely product standpoint, it looked like they were arriving late.

But what set this platform apart was its early and deliberate focus on risk maturity as a strategic pillar, not a constraint. Before a single line of code was written, the founding team included a compliance lead and a risk strategist. Together, they shaped not only the company's policies, but its architecture and product philosophy.

Unlike many fintechs, this platform launched with:

➤ Tiered onboarding flows tied to real-time risk scoring.

➤ Embedded transaction monitoring with behavioral anomaly detection

➤ Automated documentation systems for regulatory reporting

➤ A dedicated internal team responsible for maintaining a dynamic risk appetite statement, updated quarterly with executive input.

The result wasn't just lower fraud or fewer chargebacks. It was built on trust with banks, regulators, and enterprise partners.

When the company approached Tier 1 banks to negotiate access to payment rails, their documentation was clean, their metrics reliable, and their governance structure fully auditable. Instead of facing resistance, they were invited to participate in pilots, co-develop protocols, and access premium rates usually reserved for institutions twice their size.

They were also able to expand into restricted verticals, like gaming, crypto, and healthcare payments, because their internal controls exceeded regulatory expectations. While competitors scrambled to retrofit compliance after the fact, this platform had already embedded risk logic into product design.

Internally, the culture reflected the same discipline. Engineers received risk training alongside technical onboarding. Product teams worked from shared documents that included regulatory context. The fraud team wasn't tucked away in operations; it sat side-by-side with design and data science.

As the company scaled, this foundation paid off. Investors noted the platform's reliability and audit-readiness as reasons for higher valuation. Partners praised its "mature beyond its years" infrastructure. And when the regulatory environment tightened, the company didn't slow down; it accelerated.

What We Learned from Case Study 5: The Outage That Shattered Trust

Context

The platform had built its brand on reliability. It served millions of users with instant disbursements, real-time balances, and seamless integrations into marketplaces and gig platforms. Speed was the promise. "Always on" was the pitch.

Engineering had invested heavily in scalability, but incident response had never been fully stress-evaluated. The risk team had flagged concerns about visibility into vendor systems and service dependencies, but those discussions were postponed amid aggressive product timelines.

Then, on a Tuesday morning, the platform went dark.

Signals Missed

The outage began with a database lock caused by a third-party infrastructure failure. Within minutes, payouts stopped. Balance displays froze. API calls returned errors. Internally, dashboards failed, alerting systems malfunctioned, and the support team was flooded with tickets, many from large enterprise clients whose payroll runs had just vanished mid-stream.

But the real damage wasn't technical. It was communicative.

There was no coordinated incident response plan. Product, risk, legal, and comms teams weren't aligned on how to message users or each other.

For hours, users received vague status updates, or none. No timelines. No explanation.

Social media lit up with screenshots of failed transfers and angry customer posts. Several high-profile clients posted publicly about "platform instability."

Internal logs revealed no fallback communication workflows, no pre-approved messaging, and no user segmentation for critical status updates.

The incident lasted six hours. The reputational damage lasted far longer.

Consequences

News outlets picked up the story by the next day. Investor calls were filled with questions about resilience. Several key partners paused planned integrations, citing "stability concerns." And most damaging of all, enterprise clients began building backup systems and asking competitors for proposals.

Internally, the incident triggered a reckoning. Engineering had prioritized speed over observability. Comms hadn't been looped into risk discussions. And customer success had no authority to escalate directly to the incident command team.

The platform hadn't just suffered a technical failure; it had suffered a trust failure.

What Should Have Been in Place

A comprehensive incident response plan with cross-functional ownership, pre-approved messaging, and real-time decision authority.

Role-based alerts and user-tiered communication plans, ensuring that critical customers receive priority updates.

Regular crisis simulation exercises help teams understand how to respond under pressure and learn from near misses.

Clear postmortem practices, documenting what failed, what worked, and how the system will be hardened.

Reputational risk isn't about uptime. It's about how a company behaves when things go wrong, and whether users believe it's still worthy of their trust.

Takeaway

In payments, trust doesn't fail slowly. It fails instantly. And it's rebuilt not with promises, but with preparedness.

Following is the Case Study Summary: Patterns, Signals, and Lessons

Chapter Summary: Lessons Written in Hindsight

Risk frameworks are built in boardrooms, but they're evaluated in chaos. In this chapter, we stepped out of theory and into the real-world consequences of decisions made under pressure, often with incomplete information and imperfect systems. The case studies told a story not just of failures, but of patterns, the kinds of patterns that repeat across companies, markets, and business models.

We saw how a fintech's race for rapid onboarding enabled synthetic identities to drain millions in fraudulent advances. We observed a PSP lose its banking relationships due to underestimating the reputational cost of unchecked merchant practices. We followed a platform's rules engine as it crumbled under fraud strategies that had outgrown its logic. And we examined how a seemingly harmless product optimization unraveled into a multi-jurisdictional compliance breach.

But we also saw what it looks like when risk is done right, when it's integrated into product decisions, operations, and culture from day one. That final case showed that managing risk isn't just about prevention; it's about positioning. It can open doors, attract better partners, and differentiate a platform in a sea of competitors.

The through line is clear: risk is not a post-mortem exercise. It is a living part of the business. Ignored, it grows quietly. Managed well, it becomes a force multiplier.

The goal of these stories is not to scare you, but to prepare you, to provide reference points when you face similar decisions. Because you will, and the outcome will depend not on luck, but on readiness.

Chapter 11: Building a Scalable Risk Strategy

By now, one thing should be clear: risk isn't a switch you flip. It's a system you grow.

It starts small, with a few basic checks, a spreadsheet of flagged users, and a weekly review meeting. But as a payments business gains momentum, so does its risk surface: more users, more partners, more markets, more features. What worked for a team of five becomes fragile for a team of fifty. The ad hoc controls, reactive reviews, and static dashboards lack scalability.

That's why risk strategy must evolve alongside the business. And not just in scope, in structure, ownership, and speed. A scalable risk strategy isn't about doing more. It's about doing the right things, automated where possible, prioritized by impact, and designed for longevity.

In this chapter, we move from case studies to construction. We'll explore how high-performing payment organizations build risk strategies that don't just catch issues; they enable growth by making the company more trustworthy, more agile, and more resilient.

We'll break this down into core components:

➢ How to define a dynamic risk appetite that evolves with product and market expansion.

➢ How to build a risk operations function that scales with volume without collapsing under alerts

➢ How to align engineering, product, and compliance under shared goals and shared accountability

➢ How to measure risk not just in losses, but in business enablement

➢ Risk isn't a department. It's an operating principle.

Let's begin with the foundational question every scaling company must answer: What is our risk appetite, and who decides?

Defining Risk Appetite: Balancing Act

Every company has a risk appetite, whether they've defined it or not. It's embedded in decisions: what customers they accept, what geographies they enter, how fast they move, and how much they verify. The danger lies in operating without alignment, when one team builds for scale while another quietly absorbs the risk.

A formal risk appetite statement is more than a compliance exercise. It's a directional anchor, a declaration of how much risk the business is willing to accept, in what areas, and under what conditions. And like any anchor, it must be solid, but it must also be flexible enough to move with the tides.

For example, a startup offering instant payouts to gig workers might accept higher fraud exposure early on, prioritizing user acquisition. But as volume grows and partnerships deepen, that tolerance must narrow, or the very model that enabled growth will threaten its sustainability.

The process of defining risk appetite starts with executive ownership. This can't be a policy written by a single risk officer or compliance lead. It must be sponsored by leadership, often at the board level, and agreed upon across functions. Finance must understand the cost implications. Product must align incentives. Operations must know where the red lines are.

But writing the statement is only the first step. The real power comes from embedding it into decision-making. Risk appetite must influence product development, merchant underwriting, KYC thresholds, and fraud model tuning. It should shape how edge cases are managed and when exceptions are escalated.

And it must evolve. Risk appetite is not fixed. It shifts with market conditions, regulatory changes, funding stages, or customer mixes. A company entering a new vertical may choose to expand its appetite, while a firm facing increased scrutiny might tighten controls across the board.

The best organizations don't view this as a constraint. They see it as clarity, a shared understanding that enables faster, more consistent decisions. Teams no longer debate blindly over whether a feature is "too risky." They reference a framework that defines what's acceptable, what's not, and when to ask for exceptions.

In essence, defining risk appetite is about answering this question: How much uncertainty are we willing to carry, and why?

With that foundation in place, the next challenge is execution: building the operations function that brings risk strategy to life without bottlenecking growth.

Scaling Risk Operations Without Slowing Down

As a payments business grows, so does its exposure: more customers, more transactions, more edge cases, more fraud attempts, more compliance demands. At some point, spreadsheets and Slack channels aren't enough. That's when companies realize you don't just need a risk strategy; you need a risk operations engine.

Risk operations are the connective tissue between policy and practice. It's the team that turns risk appetite into workflows, metrics, and interventions. Done well, it enables growth. Done poorly, it becomes a bottleneck, slow, reactive, and overloaded with false positives.

The challenge is to scale this function without stalling innovation. That means designing risk ops for efficiency, context, and adaptability.

At early stages, one or two analysts may review flags manually, handle disputes, and escalate suspicious activity. But this model doesn't last. As transaction volume climbs, human triage becomes unscalable, and burnout is inevitable. The transition requires not just headcount, but structure.

That structure often includes:

➢ A centralized case management system that captures alerts, actions, and outcomes

➢ Tiered queues that route high-risk cases to specialists and automate low risk approvals.

➢ Playbooks that define standard actions for common scenarios, not as rigid scripts, but as decision support tools

➢ Feedback loops between fraud analysts, product teams, and engineers to continually tune rules and models.

But scaling isn't just about process. It's about clarity. Who owns what? How quickly should cases be resolved? What happens when a user is flagged? Risk ops teams must define and track service-level agreements (SLAs), escalation paths, and decision rights, or chaos ensues.

One of the most common pitfalls is failing to invest in tools. Teams that rely on generic CRMs or outdated ticketing systems quickly hit friction: every extra click, manual export, or context switch compounds over thousands of interactions. The most effective risk operations environments are purpose-built, tightly integrated with fraud engines, onboarding flows, and compliance systems.

And just as importantly, these tools must be paired with training and context. A well-tuned queue means nothing if analysts don't understand the underlying risks. Teams require access to data, a clear understanding of business priorities, and the ability to identify and raise red flags when the system itself becomes part of the problem.

In short, scaling risk operations is not about handling more; it's about managing smarter. It's about automation where it helps, judgment where it matters, and visibility at every step.

Because if your business is growing and your risk team is just getting louder, not faster, not clearer, not more aligned, you don't have scale. You have a strain.

Aligning Risk, Product, and Engineering

One of the most persistent challenges in scaling risk is also one of the most avoidable: misalignment between risk, product, and engineering. These teams often work in parallel, chasing different goals, speaking different languages, and measuring success in incompatible ways.

The result? Risk feels like a blocker. Product feels like a liability. Engineering gets stuck in the middle, patching urgent fires instead of building long-term solutions. And decisions that should be collaborative become adversarial.

This divide isn't caused by malice. It's usually a structural issue, a legacy of how companies grow. Risk starts as a compliance requirement, not a strategic function. Product ships fast and breaks things. Engineering builds to spec. And by the time risk incidents start piling up, the gap has hardened into a cultural rift.

Fixing it requires more than cross-functional meetings. It demands a shift in how ownership, incentives, and priorities are defined across the company.

At high-performing organizations, risk is treated not as a siloed team, but as a shared responsibility:

➢ Product managers are trained in core risk concepts and help define guardrails, not just features.

➢ Risk teams are embedded early in product discovery, not looped in post-launch.

➢ Engineers have visibility into fraud patterns, compliance obligations, and technical debt related to risk systems.

This alignment starts with shared language. Risk teams must learn to speak in terms of product velocity and user experience. Product teams must understand the operational cost of fraud, the weight of regulatory scrutiny, and the trade-offs involved in every edge case they enable.

And most importantly, they must share a standard definition of success. A feature that drives growth but increases disputes is not a win. A rule that reduces fraud but cuts conversion by 15% is not a solution. Alignment means optimizing together, through experimentation, simulation, and iteration.

Companies that get this right often build joint scorecards, blending metrics like fraud rates, dispute volumes, false positives, and conversion. They celebrate when fraud drops without hurting user experience, or when a compliance feature gets adopted seamlessly because it was built into the product, not bolted on.

The best risk controls don't feel like controls at all; they think like product features. Invisible, intuitive, and aligned with the user's intent. But they only happen when risk, product, and engineering are built not in sequence, but coordinated.

Measuring Risk as a Strategic Input

Most companies treat risk as something to be minimized. But the most resilient organizations treat it as something to be measured, understood, and used, not just to prevent losses, but to shape strategy.

The traditional way of thinking about risk metrics is reactive: the number of fraud cases, the amount lost, chargeback rates, compliance exceptions, and alerts triggered. These are important, but they only tell half the story —the part that comes after the damage has been done.

A scalable risk strategy requires a shift: from reactive metrics to strategic indicators. These are signals that help companies see around corners, anticipate exposure, and evaluate the cost of growth in real time.

For example:

> A spike in newly onboarded users with incomplete profiles may signal synthetic fraud or broken UX.

> A rise in dispute rates after a product change may reflect unclear billing descriptors or deceptive merchant practices.

➤ An increase in manual reviews may point to over-restrictive rules or a blind spot in automated scoring.

These aren't just operational signals. They're business insights. They inform leadership about strained systems, eroding user trust, and product incentives that create downstream problems. When tracked consistently, they become inputs for roadmap prioritization, resourcing, and even pricing strategy.

But to be useful, risk metrics must be understood outside the risk team. Executives need clarity, not jargon. Product needs context, not compliance checklists. That means designing dashboards and reporting frameworks that tie risk data to strategic goals, not just operational performance.

Instead of "fraud rate," talk about revenue at risk. Instead of "KYC drop-off," talk about conversion losses due to friction. Translate the language of loss into the language of trade-offs.

And most importantly, companies must measure not just the downside of risk, but the upside of good risk management. How many high-risk users were safely approved due to better controls? How much faster was the regulatory review because the documentation was clean?

How many markets were entered successfully because compliance was built in from day one?

Risk is not just the cost of doing business. It's the signal that shapes how business gets done. Measured well, it becomes a strategic lever, one that guides smarter decisions, sharper focus, and more sustainable growth.

Chapter Summary: Risk That Grows With You

Risk management at scale is not about saying "no" more often; it's about saying "yes" more confidently. It's about creating a structure where decisions are not slowed by fear but accelerated by clarity. Where product teams innovate with context, and operations scale with precision. Where the business moves fast and smart.

This chapter reframes risk not as a defensive function, but as a scalable asset. We explored how defining risk appetite creates a common understanding of what matters and what the business can tolerate. We looked at how to build and empower risk operations to keep pace with growth, not just fighting fires but building systems that adapt. We saw how cross-functional alignment breaks down silos and turns tension into partnership. And we examined how metrics, when measured thoughtfully, turn risk into a lens for strategic insight, not just incident response.

Because growth doesn't reduce risk, it multiplies it. And the only way to keep up is to design for it, structurally, culturally, and systemically.

The most successful payment companies aren't the ones that avoid risk altogether. They're the ones that understand it, own it, and evolve with it. They treat risk as a first-class citizen, not a last-minute fix.

And when that happens, risk management doesn't just protect the business. It propels it.

Chapter 12: The Future of Risk in Payments

Risk in payments has never stood still. It has evolved with every shift in consumer behavior, every leap in technology, and every change in regulatory philosophy. What once centered around bounced checks and stolen cards has transformed into a complex, global matrix of synthetic identities, algorithmic fraud, decentralized finance, and real-time compliance demands.

And the next wave is already here.

This chapter looks ahead. Not as a prediction, but as a provocation. What risks will define the next decade of payments? Which systems will hold, and which will break under new pressure? How can organizations prepare for a landscape shaped not by rules alone, but by data, AI, automation, and fragmentation?

We'll explore:

➢   The rise of AI-powered fraud, both for attackers and defenders

➢   The decentralization of financial infrastructure through crypto and embedded finance

➢   The impact of real-time everything, from payments to compliance to investigations

➢ How regulation is shifting from prescriptive to

➢ Why digital identity, not just KYC, will become the next big battleground.

➢ And how trust, transparency, and resilience will define the next generation of market leaders.

The companies that succeed in this new era won't be the ones that follow rules. They'll be the ones that adapt fast, design with risk in mind, and treat resilience as a product feature.

Let's begin by examining one of the most disruptive forces on the horizon: the use of artificial intelligence on both sides of the fraud war.

AI and Risk: Smarter Fraud, Smarter Defense

Artificial Intelligence isn't coming to payments risk management; it's already here. But what makes this moment different is not the technology itself. It's the asymmetry: the same tools that risk teams are beginning to use for detection and defense are also being adopted, faster and more creatively, by fraudsters.

We are entering an arms race defined not by policies or permissions, but by models, data, and speed.

On the offensive side, fraud is no longer just opportunistic; it's adaptive, distributed, and learning in real time. Generative AI allows attackers to:

➢ Forge hyper-realistic documents, voices, and biometric data with stunning accuracy.

➢ Write phishing emails indistinguishable from legitimate communications.

➢ Automate social engineering attacks at scale using personalized language scraped from the open web.

➢ Orchestrate bot-driven credential stuffing and account takeovers at scale, guided by reinforcement learning models that evaluate variables across thousands of iterations.

These are no longer isolated incidents. Fraud rings now operate like agile startups, with experimentation frameworks, version control, and their form of A/B testing to optimize attack vectors across platforms.

At the same time, traditional defenses, rule-based engines, manual reviews, and reactive alerts are proving insufficient. Static models struggle to keep pace with dynamic attackers who pivot faster than most organizations can update their workflows. This is where

AI must do more than keep pace. It must predict, prioritize, and pre-empt.

On the defensive side, risk teams are beginning to unlock new capabilities through AI:

➤ Trained on billions of transactions, it can flag subtle behavioral shifts a human would never catch.

➤ Helps link accounts, devices, and behaviors across merchants, products, and even geographies.

➤ Powers intelligent monitoring of customer support chats, refund requests, and complaint trends to spot abuse patterns

➤ Can summarize cases, suggest decisions, and route to the right analysts based on historical resolution data.

But implementing AI responsibly is a strategy. There are challenges of bias, explainability, regulatory scrutiny, and the very real risk of over-reliance. A model may spot a signal, but if no one understands why it flagged it, decisions become opaque and potentially indefensible.

Forward-looking platforms are building hybrid models, AI to surface insights, and humans-in-the-loop to validate, learn, and feed the feedback back into the system. They are treating fraud modeling like a product, with version control, experimentation environments, and impact reviews.

And significantly, they are investing in AI governance. This includes maintaining model documentation, audit trails, and fairness metrics, not because regulators demand it (yet), but because trust requires transparency, and high-stakes systems need clarity even under pressure.

This era isn't about automating risk away. It's about making risk systems faster, more intelligent, and more adaptive than the threats they face. The companies that win won't just deploy AI, they'll design ecosystems that evolve with it, integrating people, models, and feedback loops into a cohesive, responsive engine.

Because as fraud becomes smarter, defense must become strategic, not just technical.

Decentralization

For most of modern financial history, payments infrastructure was built on centralization: regulated banks, clearinghouses, and card networks operated as hubs of trust and control. But the last decade has introduced a powerful counterforce, decentralization.

It didn't start with crypto. The real fragmentation began when embedded finance allowed software companies to act like financial institutions. Marketplaces became lenders. Messaging apps became wallets. Rideshare companies started issuing cards. In parallel, open banking rules pushed traditional financial institutions to expose data and services to third parties, effectively breaking the monopoly on customer interfaces.

Then came crypto, not just as a new asset class, but as a completely different model of financial movement, where value transfer didn't require a central authority at all. Stablecoins now move billions daily across decentralized rails like Ethereum and Solana, settling in seconds without touching a traditional bank.

The result? Payments are no longer happening in one place. They're happening everywhere, all at once, across fragmented systems with differing levels of control, transparency, and risk.

This creates a massive opportunity, but also new and unpredictable risk exposures:

➤ In decentralized ecosystems, there's no central fraud team. If a user loses funds due to a smart contract vulnerability, the only recourse may be to modify the code.

➤ In embedded finance, the company offering the service may not fully understand the compliance obligations it's inheriting or may rely too heavily on a third-party Banking-as-a-Service (BaaS) provider to manage it.

> In open banking, every new connection point becomes an attack surface, especially when APIs are rushed to market or insufficiently evaluated.

What's more, these models often rely on composite service chains. A single transaction might involve an app, a wallet provider, a card processor, a bank sponsor, a compliance API, and a cloud-hosted ledger, all operated by separate companies, sometimes across borders.

In this world, risk is no longer something you manage within your infrastructure. It's something you manage across infrastructure, and often without complete visibility.

This presents new challenges for governance:

> Who is responsible when something goes wrong?

> How do you assess risk when your counterparties are updating code weekly?

> What does "compliance" look like when traditional frameworks haven't caught up to new flows?

Regulators are already grappling with these questions. In the EU and UK, embedded finance players are being scrutinized for their roles as de facto financial service providers, even when they operate behind BaaS layers. In the U.S., the Office of the Comptroller of the Currency (OCC) and the CFPB are turning their attention to oversight gaps in fintech stacks that blur accountability.

But regulation will always lag innovation. That's why companies need to engineer for resilience, not just compliance.

That means:

➢ Mapping out every dependency in your payment stack

➢ Validating the risk posture and regulatory exposure of every third-party service

➢ Designing kill-switches, redundancy protocols, and data access controls

➢ And above all, understanding that it's a redistribution of responsibility.

Some of the most forward-thinking payment providers are building "programmable trust" layers, smart contracts, identity attestations, and decentralized compliance logs that offer provable integrity across a fragmented ecosystem. Others are experimenting with regulatory nodes, where real-time compliance data is shared securely with regulators, creating a new kind of transparency by design.

In the future, centralization and decentralization won't be either/or. There'll be a spectrum, and every payment company will have to decide where it wants to sit based on its values, customers, and risk tolerance.

But one thing is sure: the days of one-size-fits-all infrastructure is over. Risk management in this new era means managing interconnection, opacity, and interdependence, without assuming someone else is in charge.

Real-Time Everything

Modern payments no longer move at the speed of business. They move faster. In an era of real-time transfers, instant settlements, and on demand everything, the very concept of latency, once a technical limitation, has become a competitive disadvantage. But speed comes at a cost: the faster a transaction happens, the less time there is to stop it.

This shift toward real-time is not limited to how funds move. It affects every layer of the payment stack: user authentication, transaction authorization, fraud detection, compliance screening, and customer resolution. What used to take hours or days is now expected to happen within milliseconds.

Consider what this means for risk operations:

➢   There's no longer a batch window to review high-risk activity before it settles.

➢   There's no buffer to reverse a suspicious payment if it's already been redeemed into crypto or cashed out via a prepaid debit card.

➢   There's no delay to observe behavior over time; the behavior is in the moment.

This has created what we might call the risk compression paradox: the better and faster the customer experience, the less time the platform has to intervene when something goes wrong.

Legacy controls, even well-tuned ones, struggle under these conditions. A rules engine designed to flag anomalies after the fact is of limited use when the money is already gone. Manual reviews become irrelevant. Escalation workflows can't keep up.

To survive in this environment, platforms must design for proactive, predictive risk, not just reactive cleanup.

Leading companies are adapting in several ways:

➤ Deploying programs that analyze user behavior in real-time and score transactions before authorization completes.

➤ Integrating policies directly into the payment flow, rather than relying on post-settlement review

➤ Shifting from static rules to dynamic, where contextual signals (device shifts, IP anomalies, behavioral patterns) trigger dynamic risk-based responses, such as multi-factor prompts, transaction delays, or feature throttling

But real-time doesn't just require technical upgrades. It demands organizational readiness. Risk teams must have the authority to act without bureaucratic delays. Engineers must prioritize uptime *and* rollback strategies. Customer service must be equipped to manage spikes in edge cases with empathy and accuracy, because real-time systems amplify the cost of bad experiences.

The expectations are unforgiving. Customers don't just expect money to move instantly; they expect errors to be fixed instantly, too. But while speed is binary for users, it's multi-dimensional for platforms. They must process, detect, and resolve faster, all without compromising control.

In this reality, risk doesn't just ride alongside the business. It must be embedded in the pulse of every real-time decision. Every transaction becomes a judgment call. Every millisecond matters. And every delay or false flag shapes the user's trust.

Real-time risk is not just about velocity. It's about precision under pressure. And in the future, those who master this balance will win, not because they're the fastest, but because they're the most adaptive.

Outcomes-Based Regulation and Compliance

For decades, financial regulation was a checklist. If you followed the rules, filed the reports, and passed the audits, you were compliant. But the world of payments has changed, and regulators are changing with it. Increasingly, we are entering an era of outcomes-based regulation, where results matter more than procedures, and intent is measured by impact.

This shift has profound implications.

Outcomes-based regulation means regulators are no longer satisfied with whether a company has controls.

They want to know if those controls work. Are you preventing fraud? Are you enabling safe access to financial services? Are your dispute processes fair, your disclosures clear, your sanctions compliance airtight?

It's not about checking the right boxes; it's about achieving the proper outcomes.

Consider the evolution in AML enforcement. It's no longer sufficient to show that you have transaction monitoring rules and SAR filing processes. Regulators now ask: how many suspicious users slipped through? What percentage of alerts result in real findings? How quickly can you detect anomalies, and how effectively do you escalate them?

Similarly, in the realm of consumer protection, regulators don't just want to see disclosure templates. They ask: Do users understand what they're signing up for? Are dispute resolutions consistent and timely? Are customers disproportionately harmed by unclear fee structures or automated denials?

This represents a deeper accountability, one that many fintechs are not yet prepared for.

Outcomes-based regulation also reflects a broader truth: technology outpaces policy. No regulator can write a detailed rule for every possible fraud vector, financial product, or onboarding model. Instead, they're focusing on principles: transparency, fairness, harm reduction, systemic integrity.

This shift creates both risk and opportunity.

The risk is ambiguity. Without clear rules, companies may struggle to understand expectations and may under- or over-comply as a result. It requires more decisive internal judgment, documentation, and culture.

But the opportunity is enormous. Companies that build risk and compliance frameworks based on performance, not just policy, can innovate faster, win regulator trust, and enter new markets with confidence. They treat audits as milestones, not minefields. They design risk systems not just to catch bad actors, but to prove effectiveness.

Forward-thinking platforms are now:

➢   Building compliance dashboards that track not just task completion, but (e.g., time-to-flag, false positive rate, consumer redress latency)

➢   Creating review control outcomes quarterly, with board-level visibility

➤ Investing in data proactively and demonstrating readiness before mandates arrive

Some are even building internal regulatory simulations, sandboxing new products against compliance goals, testing policies in synthetic environments, and documenting not just what they do, but *why* it works.

Outcomes-based regulation doesn't mean regulation is going away. It means accountability is evolving. Compliance is no longer a matter of meeting minimum standards; it's a matter of proving you can operate responsibly in complex, high-speed, and high-impact environments.

The companies that thrive in this new landscape will do more than stay out of trouble. They'll turn compliance into confidence, for users, for partners, and regulators alike.

Digital Identity as the New Risk Frontier

If data is the currency of the digital economy, then identity is the vault, and increasingly, the battleground. In payments, identity is more than just who someone is. It's how they're verified, how they access services, and how trust is extended, or denied, across platforms. And in an era of synthetic fraud, decentralized systems, and remote everything, the old models of identity are breaking down.

Traditional KYC processes were built for a world of face-to-face onboarding and regulated intermediaries. Show your ID. Sign a form. Pass a background check. But today, users can sign up for financial services from anywhere, using any device, often with nothing more than a phone number and a selfie. The explosion of digital onboarding has unlocked scale but also invited new forms of identity abuse.

Synthetic identity fraud, where fraudsters blend real and fake information to create new personas, is now one of the fastest-growing forms of financial crime. It's hard to detect because these personas often look legitimate. They pass credit checks. They behave normally. And then they default, disappear, or get used as mules in broader financial crime networks.

But even legitimate users present new challenges. People don't have a single identity. They have multiple fragments: emails, usernames, device fingerprints, IPs, social handles, and payment tokens. Stitching these together accurately, without mistaking the same person for two or mistaking two people for one, is increasingly a core function of risk.

This is why many forward-thinking platforms now treat identity infrastructure as foundational to their business, not just a compliance requirement. They're moving beyond static verification and embracing dynamic identity models, systems that learn, adapt, and build profiles over time based on behavior, device usage, geolocation, and interaction history.

Some are integrating with global digital ID networks, allowing users to port identity credentials across services, reducing friction and fraud simultaneously. Others are building internal identity graphs, mapping the relationships between users, accounts, devices, and transactions to detect anomalies and prevent manipulation.

But this shift introduces new responsibilities. Identity data is among the most sensitive information a company can store. With great power comes enormous privacy risk. Companies must design systems that are not only effective but also ethically sound. That means:

Offering users transparency into how identity data is used.

Building consent mechanisms that go beyond checkbox compliance.

Designing fallback paths for users who fail automated verification, to avoid excluding the very people financial services are meant to include.

We're also seeing identity become programmable. In blockchain ecosystems, users can own and manage their identity credentials through self-sovereign identity (SSI) solutions. These allow verification without disclosing personal information, for example, proving you're over 18 without sharing your birthdate. While early, this model hints at a future where trust is portable and privacy-preserving verification is the norm.

For risk professionals, the takeaway is clear: in the coming years, identity won't just be an input to risk models, it will be the risk model. The ability to confidently and continuously answer the question "Who is this, and what should they be allowed to do?" will determine not just fraud outcomes, but user experience, regulatory exposure, and platform credibility.

The next frontier isn't detecting fraud after it happens. It's understanding who you're dealing with before anything happens at all.

Resilience, Trust, and the New Definition of Success

In a world where money moves faster than ever and threats evolve by the hour, the most important metric for a payments company is no longer growth. It's resilience. Not just how fast you can scale, but how well you can absorb shocks, detect anomalies, correct mistakes, and earn trust in the face of uncertainty.

Resilience is the ability to take a hit, such as a fraud wave, a compliance inquiry, or a system outage, and not just survive, but learn. It's not about eliminating risk, but absorbing it in a way that protects customers, partners, and the long-term viability of the business.

In the past, resilience was an infrastructure term, including data centers, failover protocols, and uptime SLAs. But in today's risk environment, resilience is cross-functional:

➤ Legal teams must respond quickly to changing regulatory expectations.

➤ Fraud teams must tune models with new data faster than bad actors evolve.

➤ Product teams must design features that degrade gracefully, not catastrophically.

➢ Customer service must be empowered to repair trust, not just resolve tickets.

And above all, leadership must embrace the idea that resilience is proactive. It is built in advance, in how teams are structured, how systems are architected, and how decisions are made under pressure.

But resilience alone isn't enough. The real differentiator in the coming decade will be trust.

Trust is the currency of digital finance. It determines whether users sign up, whether regulators engage constructively, and whether partners are willing to take a bet on your platform. And trust is fragile; it can be lost in a single breach, a single headline, or a single overlooked signal.

Building trust requires transparency. That means:

➢ Giving users clear, honest communication about their data and their rights

➢ Explaining decisions made by automated systems, and offering paths for recourse

➢ Demonstrating to regulators not just that your controls exist, but that they're practical, measurable, and evolving.

> ➢ And trust requires consistency. Risk cannot be something you fix when it breaks. It must be.

So, what does success in payments risk look like now?

It's not just about fraud rates. It's about how quickly you can respond when the unexpected happens. It's not just about staying out of trouble; it's about being invited into rooms because your reputation for responsibility precedes you. It's not just about compliance, it's about credibility.

The most valuable platforms in the next wave of digital finance will not be those that grew the fastest. They will be those who understood their risks early, adapted quickly, and trusted their operating system.

Because in the end, success isn't measured in transaction volume or valuations. It's measured in how much people are willing to bet on your ability to keep their money and their trust safe.

Chapter Summary: Navigating the Horizon

The future of payments risk isn't a single threat or technology. It's a landscape, fast-moving, interconnected, and perpetually unfinished. As new tools emerge and systems evolve, so too does the surface area for risk. What once were edge cases are now everyday realities. What once took days to detect must now be caught in milliseconds. And what once defined success, growth at all costs, has given way to a more urgent question: can you scale trust as fast as you scale revenue?

This chapter explored that shift.

We examined how AI is both a weapon and a shield, enabling smarter fraud but also powering the next generation of defense. We looked at decentralization and the fragmentation of infrastructure, where risk is no longer housed in a single platform but flows across networks of interdependent services. We explored the challenge of real-time everything, where decisions must be made before the threat fully reveals itself.

We saw how regulators are shifting from rule-based checklists to outcomes-based accountability, demanding not just activity, but results. And we explored how digital identity is becoming the new battleground, not just for verification, but for inclusion, privacy, and control.

And finally, we returned to first principles: resilience and trust. Because in the end, the platforms that endure will be the ones that can adapt under pressure, communicate with clarity, and uphold credibility even when everything around them is shifting.

The next decade will not reward those who try to outrun risk. It will reward those who build with risk in mind from the beginning, who treat it not as a cost to minimize but as a capability to master.

This isn't just the future of risk. It's the future of leadership in payments.

Chapter 13: Risk Management to Risk Leadership

Risk management is no longer a back-office function. In today's payments ecosystem, it is a core lever of strategy, a driver of trust, and a visible signal of maturity. And for those who understand how to wield it, it becomes a competitive advantage.

Throughout this book, we've examined how risk plays out in real time: through systems, decisions, failures, frameworks, and recoveries. But risk doesn't just shape transactions; it shapes leadership. Because the best leaders in payments aren't just those who grow fast, they're those who grow responsibly, recover gracefully, and adapt endlessly.

This final chapter is not about controls. It's about mindset.

It asks: What does it take to lead in a risk-defined world? How can individuals and organizations elevate risk from an operational necessity to a cultural cornerstone? And what happens when companies stop asking, "How do we avoid risk?" and start asking, "How do we lead with it?"

We'll explore:

➢ The difference between risk and risk

➢ How to create a culture where risk is everyone's job, not just the second line's

➢ What it means to be transparent about mistakes and learn in public

➢ How to design executive decision-making structures that reflect both speed and accountability.

➢ And why the next generation of fintech leaders will be those who treat trust, transparency, and long-term resilience as primary success metrics.

This is not the end of risk; it's the beginning of risk leadership.

Let's start with the most foundational shift: transforming risk from a department into a shared discipline.

From Function to Culture: Making Risk Everyone's Job

In many organizations, risk often resides in a corner, as a compliance checklist, a review queue, or a final sign-off before launch. It's treated as a function. A box. A hurdle to clear. But in the most resilient, forward-thinking payments companies, risk doesn't belong to one team. It belongs to everyone.

Risk leadership begins when companies stop thinking of risk as a department and start treating it as a culture, a shared lens through which every decision is made, from engineering to marketing, product to partnerships.

This doesn't mean every employee needs to be an expert in fraud patterns or regulatory statutes. It means every employee understands the stakes of what they're building. It means that when a new feature is proposed, someone asks, "What could go wrong, and how do we catch it early?" It means that risk is part of product discovery, not just QA. That analysts and engineers collaborate, not compete. That compliance teams help guide innovation, not block it.

In a risk-driven culture:

➢ Product managers are rewarded not just for launching fast, but for launching with controls embedded and edge cases evaluated.

➢ Engineers write code with failure paths in mind, not just the happy path.

➢ Designers understand how friction, used well, can prevent abuse or increase clarity.

➢ Customer support is empowered to flag suspicious trends before they escalate into patterns.

And leadership listens. Not just when something breaks, but as part of an ongoing dialogue between risk and growth, control and ambition.

This culture isn't built overnight. It requires:

➤ Giving teams the language, context, and case studies to recognize risk signals before they escalate

➤ Measuring and rewarding risk-aware behavior, not just top-line KPIs

➤ Making risk metrics as visible as revenue dashboards because what's measured shapes what's prioritized.

➤ Encouraging people to raise concerns without fear of retribution, even when the answer is "we're not sure yet"

Some companies codify this into rituals: quarterly risk reviews that include all departments; pre-mortem sessions before big launches; open retrospectives after incidents to discuss what went wrong, and how to learn without blame.

When risk is cultural, teams don't just respond faster. They build better. They anticipate more. They reduce fragility at the root. And they stop seeing risk as the thing that slows them down and start seeing it as the thing that keeps them moving forward with confidence.

Because the truth is simple: in a risk-defined world, everyone's job is risk. And leadership means making sure they know it and are equipped to act on it.

Transparency, Accountability, and Learning in Public

In traditional financial services, risk is something to hide. Problems are buried in legal language. Breaches are disclosed at the last possible moment. Failures are downplayed, or worse, ignored. But in the new era of payments, transparency is not a liability. It's a leadership trait.

Customers expect more. So do regulators. And so does the market.

Today, companies that own their mistakes early, openly, and constructively don't lose trust. They earn more of it. Not because they're perfect, but because they're honest, responsive, and focused on doing better.

Transparency in risk leadership means moving beyond a reactive posture. It means:

> ➤ Telling users not just what happened, but what you're doing about it.

> ➤ Publishing your security principles, not just your privacy policy

> ➤ Explaining your fraud controls to partners and inviting them to shape best practices.

> ➤ Being honest with investors about losses, risk exposures, and what's being done to improve them.

This doesn't mean exposing every internal system or tactic. But it does mean cultivating a public posture that says: we take risk seriously, and we take responsibility when things go wrong.

That sense of responsibility also applies internally. In many organizations, the fear of blame stifles progress. When something fails, whether it's a missed alert, a bad call, or a system gap, the instinct is to isolate the incident, contain the fallout, and move on. But when risk is seen as a learning opportunity, not a career-ending error, the organization gets smarter.

Companies that lead with risk create space for:

> ➤ Where the goal is insight, not indictment.

➤ Where teams share failures so others can learn without repeating them

➤ Documenting what went wrong so that controls can be improved before disaster strikes.

This culture of learning in public extends beyond the company walls. Some of the most respected platforms publish risk whitepapers, release transparency reports, and contribute to open-source fraud tools, not as PR exercises, but as acts of ecosystem stewardship. They recognize that raising the bar on risk across the industry protects everyone, including themselves.

Transparency and accountability aren't about perfection. They're about earning the right to operate and to lead.

Eventually, the companies that survive aren't the ones that avoid every mistake. They're the ones who manage mistakes with clarity, integrity, and speed.

Because in payments, as in leadership, how you respond matters as much as what went wrong.

Redefining Metrics: Beyond Losses and Approvals

For years, the success of a risk team was measured by two blunt metrics: losses prevented, and fraudsters stopped. While important, these numbers only tell part of the story. They reduce risk to an expense, a necessary cost center, a firewall against worst-case scenarios.

But in the modern payments' world, this framing is outdated. Risk is no longer just a shield. It's an engine, one that shapes user experience, unlocks growth, earns regulator confidence, and determines who gets to scale.

That's why the next generation of risk leaders is redefining what they measure and what those metrics mean.

Instead of only asking "How many bad actors did we block?" they ask:

➢ How many did we allow to onboard without friction?

➢ How much did we recover by reducing false positives?

➢ How quickly did we resolve disputes, and how satisfied were the customers afterward?

➤ How many markets could we enter because our risk posture met local expectations?

➤ How did our response time to incidents improve quarter over quarter?

➤ Are our fraud models explainable enough to pass a regulatory audit?

These aren't vanity metrics. They're strategic signals. They help organizations make better decisions across product, engineering, finance, and operations. They allow teams to see not just where loss is happening, but where trust is being built or eroded.

For example, a high approval rate means nothing if it hides growing downstream losses. A low fraud rate isn't helpful if it comes at the cost of blocking thousands of legitimate customers. And a clean audit means little if internal teams don't understand how they achieved it, or how to repeat it under stress.

That's why forward-thinking companies are now creating risk scorecards that blend qualitative and quantitative inputs across teams. These scorecards track:

➤ User friction by segment

➤ Time to detect and act on anomalies.

- ➢ Cost per false positive

- ➢ Success rate of risk escalations

- ➢ Regulatory engagement velocity and outcomes

- ➢ Cultural indicators, like internal risk reporting volume and responsiveness

These scorecards are shared widely, not hidden in dashboards that only risk teams can read. They're reviewed in leadership meetings, discussed in all-hands sessions, and used to inform budgeting and prioritization. When everyone understands how risk is measured, they start contributing to its management.

The best risk metrics don't just measure defense. They enable decisions. They tell the story of how a company navigates uncertainty and protects what matters most: user trust, business integrity, and operational resilience.

In short, risk leadership means measuring what matters, not just what's easy.

The Risk Leader's Playbook

Risk leaders aren't just subject matter experts. They're system architects, cultural catalysts, and ethical stewards. They sit at the intersection of business ambition and operational reality, and they make the invisible visible. They guide not just what a company avoids, but what it chooses to become.

In the payments industry, where trust is fragile and speed is unforgiving, this role has never been more essential. Risk leaders aren't just hired to prevent losses. They're expected to enable responsible growth, defend reputation, build stakeholder confidence, and operationalize trust at scale.

So, what does it take to lead in this environment?

It starts with a clear point of view. Great risk leaders don't just enforce policies. They help define the organization's appetite for uncertainty. They ask the uncomfortable questions early:

> What are we willing to risk, and why?

> Where do we draw the line between growth and exposure?

> How will we know when something is slipping before it breaks?

But vision alone isn't enough. Great risk leaders also build systems that last:

➢ They architect feedback loops that allow signals to travel quickly across teams.

➢ They implement governance structures that scale, from incident response to board reporting.

➢ They ensure tooling is built not just for now, but for the business they want to become.

➢ And they continually evolve controls in response to threats, not to keep up with compliance, but to stay ahead of failure.

Most importantly, risk leaders create alignment. They speak the language of the business, not just controls and compliance, but revenue, churn, NPS, and velocity. They embed themselves into product and engineering. They collaborate with marketing to pre-empt reputational issues. They turn risk from an internal police force into an enabler of intelligent trade-offs.

And when things go wrong, because they will, risk leaders show up with clarity, not panic. They communicate facts. They act decisively. They maintain transparency. They protect the people affected. And they ensure that every incident leaves the company stronger than before.

There is no single path to becoming a risk leader. Some come from finance, others from operations, security, product, or policy. What they share is a mindset:

➢ One that views risk not as a barrier, but as a design constraint.

➢ One that sees users not as problems to manage, but as stakeholders to protect.

➢ One that believes the role of risk is not to slow the business down, but to enhance value.

This playbook is never finished. The threats evolve. The tools change. The structure flexes. But the principles remain:

➢ Lead with clarity.

➢ Design for resilience.

➢ Embed trust everywhere.

➢ And when in doubt, make decisions you'd be proud to defend, in public, and in hindsight.

Because in the end, risk leadership isn't just about what you stop. It's about what you make possible.

The Risk-Ready Payments Organization

The payments industry sits at the intersection of trust and transformation. Every time money moves, whether it's across a street or a continent, someone is assuming risk. Fraud, regulatory scrutiny, operational disruption, reputational fallout, competitive pressure: these forces aren't occasional visitors. They are constant companions.

But risk, when understood and managed well, isn't a threat to progress; it's the foundation that makes progress sustainable.

Throughout this book, we've explored the structures, practices, and philosophies that define modern risk management in the payment's ecosystem. From the core mechanics of compliance and fraud detection to the complexities of cross-border regulation and third-party dependencies, we've seen that risk is not one thing: it's a network of interdependent exposures. Some are obvious and immediate. Others are hidden in code, contracts, or market shifts still to come.

We examined how artificial intelligence is reshaping decision-making. Decentralized systems are challenging traditional controls, identity is becoming more personal, and encryption is becoming more vulnerable. And through it all, one truth remained clear: the companies that will succeed aren't the ones with perfect protection, they're the ones that can move with confidence in a constantly changing environment.

So, what does a risk-ready payments organization look like?

It's one where risk leadership is embedded, not isolated, participating in product sprints, go-to-market plans, and infrastructure design.

It's one where culture reinforces vigilance, where employees at every level understand their role in protecting the platform, and escalation is encouraged, not avoided.

It's one where tools support judgment, not replace it, where automation is embraced but not unquestioningly trusted, and decisions remain explainable.

It's one where governance scales with growth, not to slow things down, but to make sure they're done right.

And most of all, it's one where risk is seen as a strategic asset, not a defensive drag. The strongest payments companies are not those that avoid risk entirely, but those that understand it, own it, and turn it into an advantage.

The Risk You Choose

Payments move money. Risk shapes what moves and what breaks. But underneath every decision, every alert, every mitigation strategy, lies something more profound: a choice. Not just about what to protect, but what kind of organization you're building.

This book began with a simple premise: that risk is no longer a back-office concern. It is now a core force in strategy, trust, and innovation. Along the way, we unpacked the mechanics of fraud, compliance, cyber threats, and operational exposure. We traced real-world failures and hard-won lessons. We explored emerging threats, including AI-powered fraud, decentralized infrastructure, and compressed risk windows, and examined how leaders can respond.

But if there is one message that runs through every chapter, it's this: Risk isn't just something to manage. It's something to lead.

The payments companies that will thrive tomorrow are not the ones that grow fast. They are the ones that grow intentionally, with clear guardrails, dynamic controls, and a culture of curiosity, accountability, and trust. They will embed resilience into their DNA. They will measure not just what went wrong, but what could have gone wrong. And they will move through uncertainty not with fear, but with fluency.

Risk will never go away. It will keep multiplying. But that's not a threat. It's an invitation to lead smarter, build stronger, and operate with a deeper understanding of what it means to move money in a volatile, interconnected world.

So, whether you are a founder, an analyst, a product owner, or a regulator, remember:

You don't just inherit risk. You shape it. Choose wisely. And lead well.

Books by David Webb

The Book On Life Unscripted

The Book On Risk Management in Payments

The Book On Strategic Obsession

The Book On High-Stakes Thinking

The Book On Artificial Leverage

About the Author

David Webb is a seasoned entrepreneur and business leader with more than three decades of experience at the intersection of technology, finance, and services. As the founder and CEO of multiple ventures—some celebrated successes and some hard-learned failures—he has cultivated a reputation for turning complexity into clarity, driving growth, and leading organizations through periods of both turbulence and transformation. His career has been defined by a willingness to take calculated risks, embrace innovation, and pursue opportunities others often overlook.

David's debut book, Life Unscripted: What You Should Have Learned in High School, distilled years of professional and personal experience into a practical guide for navigating the overlooked realities of adulthood. With his second book, The Book On Risk Management in Payments, he takes a decisive step into more specialized territory. Here, he leverages his decades of leadership and industry insight to address one of the most pressing challenges in global commerce: how to anticipate threats, safeguard trust, and manage risk in a world where money moves faster than regulation. This shift—from broad life skills to the technical, high-stakes architecture of payments—marks not only the evolution of his writing but also the deepening of his mission: to equip readers with frameworks that are as pragmatic as they are forward-looking.

Beyond writing and business, David remains committed to mentoring entrepreneurs and contributing to community initiatives that promote education, resilience, and personal growth. Whether in boardrooms, classrooms, or in print, his work reflects a consistent theme: empowering others to think critically, act decisively, and build systems that endure.

About the Publisher

Welcome to The Book On Publishing

At The Book On Publishing, we believe in rewriting the rules of learning. Whether you're chasing your next big idea, building a better life, or simply curious about what should have been taught in school, you've come to the right place.

We're a platform built for dreamers, doers, and lifelong learners, offering bold, practical books and tools that empower you to take charge of your journey. From real-world skills to mindset mastery, we publish the book on what matters.

No fluff. No lectures. Just what you need to know, delivered with clarity, purpose, and a spark of curiosity.

Start exploring. Start growing. Start authoring your story.

Read more at https://thebookon.ca.

Acknowledgment of AI Assistance

Portions of this book were developed with the support of ChatGPT, an AI language model created by OpenAI. While every word has been carefully reviewed and refined by the author, ChatGPT served as a valuable tool for brainstorming, editing, and structuring ideas. Its assistance helped accelerate the creative process and bring clarity to complex topics.